DK EYEWITNESS

TOP **10**
LAS VEGAS

Top 10 Las Vegas Highlights

The Top 10 of Everything

CONTENTS

Las Vegas Area by Area

Streetsmart

Within each Top 10 list in this book, no hierarchy of quality or popularity is implied. All 10 are, in the editor's opinion, of roughly equal merit.

Throughout this book, floors are referred to in accordance with American usage; i.e., the "first floor" is at ground level.

Title page, front cover and spine *The iconic Welcome to Fabulous Las Vegas sign*
Back cover clockwise from top left *Red Rock Canyon Conservation Area; the Strip; Wynn Las Vegas; Las Vegas sign; Stratosphere Casino Hotel*

The rapid rate at which the world is changing is constantly keeping the DK Eyewitness team on our toes. While we've worked hard to ensure that this edition of Las Vegas is accurate and up-to-date, we know that opening hours alter, standards shift, prices fluctuate, places close and new ones pop up in their stead. So, if you notice we've got something wrong or left something out, we want to hear about it. Please get in touch at **travelguides@dk.com**

Welcome to
Las Vegas

Las Vegas is the most full-on, 24-hour city you could ever hope to visit. It was built as a playground of extravagant casino resorts, top shows, and fine restaurants – a place to have fun and simply forget the world that lies beyond. With DK Eyewitness Top 10 Las Vegas, it is yours to explore.

Millions of tourists pour into Las Vegas each year. The vast majority spend their time on either **the Strip** – the legendary 4-mile (6-km) stretch of Las Vegas Boulevard that is home to the largest casino resorts – or in **Downtown Las Vegas**, the original city core that has its own cluster of smaller, but arguably more characterful, casinos. However, there are also the surrounding deserts to explore, whether you just take an early-morning hike in **Red Rock Canyon** or head further afield to **Zion National Park** or the **Grand Canyon**.

It is perfectly possible to visit Las Vegas and not gamble, but there is no avoiding the **casinos**. They are at the root of everything, holding almost all the city's hotel rooms, plus its best restaurants, bars, nightclubs, theaters, and concert arenas. Above all that, the casinos simply are the quintessential sights of Las Vegas. They are the weird and wonderful structures that everyone comes to see – the giant pyramid of **Luxor**, the miniature cities of **New York-New York** and **The Venetian**, and the fairy tale castle of **Excalibur**.

Whether you're visiting for a weekend or a week, our Top 10 guide is designed to bring together the best of everything the city has to offer, from the top shows to the hottest nightclubs. The guide has useful tips throughout, from seeking out what's free to the best venues for entertainment, plus seven easy-to-follow itineraries, designed to tie together a clutch of sights in a short space of time. Add inspiring photography and detailed maps, and you've got the essential pocket-sized travel companion. **Enjoy the book, and enjoy Las Vegas.**

Clockwise from top: **Caesars Palace, Fremont Street Experience, New York-New York, Grand Canyon, Las Vegas sign, Luxor's sphinx and pyramid, interior of Cosmopolitan**

Exploring Las Vegas

The spectacle of the Strip is what makes Las Vegas such a compelling destination, so you can expect to spend most of your time there. Make sure, though, to sample Downtown, where it all began, and see the surrounding deserts. Here are some ideas for two and four days in Las Vegas.

The ARIA Express tram is the best way to reach CityCenter.

Two Days in Las Vegas

Day ❶
MORNING

Kick-start a day on the **Strip** (see pp12–13) with breakfast beside the Grand Canal of **The Venetian** (see pp16–17), before admiring the splendor of **Wynn Las Vegas** (see pp18–19). Then have an alfresco lunch at **Paris Las Vegas** (see p41).

AFTERNOON

Shop under the ever-changing skies of the **Forum Shops at Caesars** (see pp20–21), visit the Conservatory and Botanical Gardens in **Bellagio** (see pp14–15), then ride the free tram to **CityCenter** (see pp24–5). Dine in the **ARIA Resort** (see p25). Stroll past Bellagio's fountains en route to a **Cirque du Soleil** show (see pp58–9).

Day ❷
MORNING

Take a helicopter to **Grand Canyon West** (see pp30–31) and venture onto the **Skywalk**. The flight, via the **Hoover Dam** (see pp26–7), gives a real sense of the city's desert setting.

AFTERNOON

Explore **Downtown Las Vegas** (see pp22–3) and discover its past in the **Mob Museum** (see pp92–3). Stay late for the light shows at the **Fremont Street Experience** (see p91).

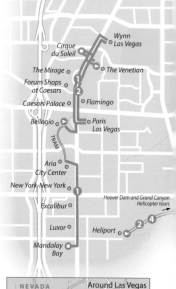

The Grand Canyon is a spectacular sight of natural beauty, easily accessible from the city.

Mob Museum
SlotZilla Zip Line
Fremont Street Experience
CAR / BUS

Key
— Two-day itinerary
— Four-day itinerary

0 meters 1000
0 yards 1000

New York-New York is a miniature Manhattan, with its own replica of Statue of Liberty.

Four Days in Las Vegas

Day ❶
MORNING
Enjoy a coffee in **Bellagio Patisserie** (see p69), then visit the **Conservatory and Botanical Gardens** (see p15), both at Bellagio. Ride the free tram to **CityCenter** (see pp24–5).
AFTERNOON
Continue to the miniature Manhattan that is **New York-New York** (see p41), the fairy tale castle of **Excalibur** (see p41), and the pyramid of the **Luxor** (see p40). Dine in **Mandalay Bay** and stay on for its nightlife.

Day ❷
MORNING
Beat the heat with an early hike at **Red Rock Canyon** (see pp28–9), continue to the **Hoover Dam** (see pp26–7), then head back for lunch at **Mon Ami Gabi** (see p68).
AFTERNOON
Stay on and explore more of **Paris Las Vegas** (see p41), then head onto other Strip highlights such as **The Venetian** (see pp16–17), and **Wynn Las Vegas** (see pp18–19). Later, catch a **Cirque du Soleil** show (see pp58–9).

Day ❸
MORNING
Cut loose on the thrill rides at **Adventuredome** and **Stratosphere Tower** (see pp52–3), or take in the wildlife at **Flamingo Las Vegas** (see p81) and **The Mirage** (see p41).
AFTERNOON
Sample **Downtown Las Vegas** (see pp22–3), zooming on the **SlotZilla Zip Line** (see p52) or visiting the **Mob Museum** (see pp92–3). See the **Fremont Street Experience** (see p91) lights.

Day ❹
MORNING
Take either a half-day excursion to **Grand Canyon West** (see pp30–31), or a full day at the **South Rim**.
AFTERNOON
Shop at **Forum Shops at Caesars** (see pp20–21). After dinner, head to **Omnia** nightclub at **Caesar's Palace** (see p40).

Top 10 Las Vegas Highlights

The atrium of The Forum Shops
at Caesars Palace

🔟 Las Vegas Highlights

The Entertainment Capital of the World offers just about everything: the world's largest hotels, the brightest stars in show business, shops and restaurants that rival any on earth. It's true, too, that the lights are brighter in Las Vegas. Yet you don't have to go far from the glamour and glitter to find the natural beauty of lakes and the desert as well.

① The Strip

The neon artery of gambling pulses with excitement. Imaginatively themed resorts make it a street that never sleeps *(see pp12–13)*.

② Bellagio

The hotel that upped the ante where Las Vegas luxury is concerned is well located, too *(see pp14–15)*.

③ The Venetian

The Italian Renaissance revisited. Minstrels and nobility stroll among Venetian landmarks as gondoliers glide by *(see pp16–17)*.

4 Wynn Las Vegas
This opulent mega-resort is set in beautiful landscaped gardens *(see pp18–19)*.

5 The Forum Shops at Caesars
The glory that was Rome provides the backdrop for a choice of upscale shops and restaurants *(see pp20–21)*.

| 0 km | 1 |
| 0 miles | 1 |

6 Downtown Las Vegas
Popularly deemed the heart of Las Vegas, the Downtown area experienced a rebirth in the late 1990s *(see pp22–3)*.

EAST BONANZA ROAD

STREET

BOULEVARD

BOULEVARD

AVENUE

AVENUE

WINCHESTER

ROAD

Las Vegas National Golf Course

SOUTH EASTERN AVENUE

SOUTH EASTERN AVE

7 CityCenter
This "city-within-a-city" is the most expensive privately funded resort complex in the United States *(see pp24–5)*.

8 Hoover Dam and Lake Mead
An engineering marvel, the dam not only tamed the Colorado River but also created Lake Mead, providing myriad aquatic pursuits, minutes from the city *(see pp26–7)*.

9 Red Rock Canyon
Though not far from the city lights, this area provides a welcome getaway from all the glitz *(see pp28–9)*.

10 Grand Canyon
The ultimate excursion from Las Vegas; whether by airplane, bus, or automobile, most visitors say the experience is unforgettable *(see pp30–31)*.

TOP 10 ⭐ The Strip

All the glamour, glitz, and glitter that epitomizes Las Vegas is concentrated along the legendary thoroughfare known simply as the Strip. This 4-mile (6-km) segment of the southern section of Las Vegas Boulevard, sufficiently far from Downtown to be outside the city's official limits, is the epicenter of the global entertainment industry, and home to many of the largest hotels and casinos on the planet. The Strip is a master of reinvention, constantly changing, surprising, and embracing new ways to impress visitors.

The Strip by Night ③

Las Vegas truly comes to life after dark **(right)**. Whether you're walking the Strip or soaring above it in a helicopter, that's when you will see the Fountains of Bellagio *(see p81)* and the Mirage Volcano *(see p83)* at their most spectacular.

① Shopping

Big-name casinos have showpiece malls – most spectacularly, Caesars Palace has The Forum Shops *(see pp20–21)* – but there are also stand-alone malls like Fashion Show *(see p72)* and The Shops at Crystals at CityCenter *(see p25)*.

④ Headliners

Since the unveiling of the Colosseum at Caesars Palace *(see p40)*, Las Vegas has resumed its role as the world's entertainment capital. Regular headliners along the Strip include Mariah Carey, Rod Stewart, and Britney Spears.

② Gambling

Gambling *(see pp56-7)* is still the bedrock on which Las Vegas rests. Whether you're hoping to beat the bank at baccarat **(below)** or predict the roulette wheel, losing can be surprisingly enjoyable.

⑤ Fine Dining

The competition between the major casinos to persuade the world's best chefs to open Las Vegas restaurants has turned the city into a foodie's dream. Current highlights are Julian Serrano *(see p66)*, Bouchon *(see p67)*, the exquisite Nobu *(see p67)*, and Scarpetta *(see p67)*.

⑥ Themed Architecture

With the Strip's inventive architecture, you can admire the world's great cities, from Paris to New York via Venice, or even time travel to ancient Rome or Egypt **(above)**.

7 Shows

Every casino-hotel along the Las Vegas Strip holds at least one theater, each hosting long-running live shows (see pp58–9) ranging from the hit comedy Menopause the Musical via magicians like Penn & Teller to the postmodern antics of the all-conquering Cirque du Soleil **(left)** and the one-of-a-kind performing arts company, the Blue Man Group.

THE MOB

As is vividly portrayed in the 1995 Robert de Niro movie Casino, organized crime and Las Vegas were natural bedfellows for several decades from the 1940s. Gangsters were drawn like magpies to the coins piling up effortlessly in so many slot machines. Bugsy Siegel was the trailblazer with his Flamingo Hotel (see p36), while Midwest crime boss Moe Dalitz opened the Desert Inn in 1950. Learn about Las Vegas's connection to the Mob and organized crime at the Mob Museum (see pp92–3).

8 Buffets

While Las Vegas does have cheap-and-cheerful buffets, upscale places like Bellagio (see pp14–15) and Wynn Las Vegas (see pp18–19) offer tempting "gourmet" options, piled with sushi, and other culinary treats.

9 Thrill Rides

A city of thrills of course comes up trumps in thrill rides. The scariest are atop Stratosphere Tower (see p87); others include the Big Apple Coaster at New York-New York **(below)** and the Adventuredome theme park at Circus Circus (see p50).

NEED TO KNOW

MAP M3–R2

Visitor information: Las Vegas Convention and Visitors Authority ■ 3150 Paradise Rd ■ 702 892 7572, 877 847 4858 ■ www.visitlasvegas.com

■ You're on vacation – why not have doughnuts for breakfast?! Delicious Krispy Kreme doughnuts are on sale at Excalibur and Circus Circus.

■ To maximize the excitement, get a hotel room with a view of the Strip. Best of all are The Venetian, Paris, and the rooms in the Luxor pyramid.

■ Be prepared to shift your body clock later than usual; Las Vegas may keep going around the clock, but the shops are the only places where there's much happening in the morning.

10 Clubbing

Casinos vie to build ever more extraordinary clubs (see pp62–3). Leading lights include Marquee, TAO Nightclub, and Encore Beach Club.

Bellagio

TOP 10 ⭐

From the flower arrangements in the halls to the fixtures in the bathtubs, Bellagio is the epitome of extravagance. The goal behind this grand monument to leisure was to create a hotel "that would exemplify absolute quality while emphasizing romance and elegance – romance in the literary sense, a place of ideal beauty and comfort; the world everyone hopes for, as it might be if everything were just right."

① **Lobby Ceiling**
Visitors are greeted by the 2,000-sq-ft (186-sq-m) glass sculpture **(left)**, the *Fiori di Como*, suspended from the lobby ceiling. The creator was Dale Chihuly, the first American artist to be designated a national living treasure. Amazingly, every single flower is different.

Via Bellagio **②**
You are only likely to frequent Bellagio's shopping promenade *(see p72)* if you have deep pockets. The boutiques are as elegant as the Via itself **(right)**, counting among them such names as Prada, Chanel, Fendi, and Gucci.

③ **Gallery of Fine Art**
Bellagio's art gallery hosts major temporary exhibitions of international artists, past and present, in conjunction with other large art galleries and museums in North America and around the world.

⑤ **Theater**
Designed for Cirque du Soleil's spectacular water-based production *O (see p58)*, the theater combines old-world magnificence (it is styled after a European opera house) with cutting-edge technology. Central to the production is an impressive 1.5-million-gallon (6.8-million-liter) pool, which can be remodeled to meet each act's needs.

Italianate Theme **④**
Fronting a pristine lake with a tree-lined boulevard beyond, this extraordinary resort hotel **(right)** was built to resemble an idyllic village on the shores of Italy's Lake Como. The theme is carried throughout the property – its original 3,000-room tower, the Spa Tower, 21 dining options, and two wedding chapels – creating an atmosphere of opulence.

6 Fountains of Bellagio

Swirling and gyrating with balletic grace, all choreographed to a booming soundtrack that ranges from Beethoven to Broadway, the fountains **(below)** in Bellagio's 8-acre (3-ha) lake spring to life every half-hour during the afternoon, and every 15 minutes after dark, providing the Strip's finest free show to the crowds that gather on the sidewalk.

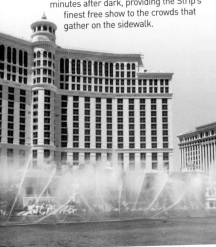

7 Conservatory and Botanical Gardens

Keen gardeners and plant-lovers will be rewarded with floral displays that change with each season and on the Chinese New Year. Each change employs the services of no fewer than 120 professionals.

8 Restaurants

Bellagio's superb restaurants include Le Cirque, Michael Mina, Noodles, Jasmine, and Yellowtail. Picasso *(see p66)* has an AAA Five Diamond Award and is decorated with originals.

9 Buffet

The Bellagio Buffet *(see p70)* has re-invented the Vegas buffet, eschewing the more common budget bonanza in favour of a gourmet spread of quality seafood and meat.

Casino 10

Less flamboyant and more sophisticated than others, this is the most aesthetically pleasing casino in Las Vegas. Slot-machine carousels **(right)** are fringed with specially designed fabrics rather than the ubiquitous neon tubing, and the custom-made carpets provide a stylish relief.

TOP 10 ★ The Venetian

Modeled on Venice, Italy, The Venetian is a massive, award-winning property. This all-suite hotel forms a mega-resort with the adjoining Palazzo, and makes an ideal base for exploring the sights of the Strip. The Grand Canal Shoppes, a mall complete with gondolas and singing gondoliers, all set against the backdrop of St. Mark's Square, offers plentiful shopping, and the gaming rooms and lavish spa are also noteworthy. There are also more than 30 fine-dining restaurants and three theaters.

1 Architecture and Ambience
The grandeur of Venice meets Las Vegas glitz, and the results are surprisingly spectacular **(above)**. True, the hotel's Grand Canal is only 1,200-ft (365-m) long as opposed to the original's 2.5 miles (4 km), but any lack of authenticity is more than made up for by the festive Las Vegas ambience.

4 Grand Canal
The Venetian has its very own Wedding Gondola **(above)** to hire for marriage ceremonies. You can even sail under the Rialto Bridge.

3 Grand Colonnade
Reproductions of frescoes framed in 24-karat gold adorn the domed and vaulted ceilings **(left)**. Marble floors, Classical columns, costumed courtiers, and a giant overview of the real Venice all serve to transport the imagination to Italy.

St. Mark's Square 2
So the geography isn't exactly as per the original, but even if you notice you probably won't care – the total effect is extremely aesthetically pleasing, perhaps more so than at any of the other resorts **(right)**.

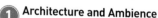

6 The Grand Canal Shoppes at The Venetian

The galaxy of goodies in the shops along the canal *(see p73)* satisfy a wide range of tastes: there are magic tricks at Houdini's and cookies and cakes at Carlo's Bakery; there is jewelry at Belluso and smart sportswear at Banana Republic. Travel the canal by gondola or meander the walkway linking the stores.

7 Restaurants

Stars of The Venetian's gastronomic line-up include celebrity restauranteur Wolfgang Puck's CUT, Timon Balloo's Sugarcane, TAO Asian Bistro, and Thomas Keller's Bouchon. You can even dine alfresco in St. Mark's Square to re-create the grand Venetian experience.

HIGH HURDLES

The journey of a major hotel-casino from the drawing board to the grand opening is a long and often tortuous process. Of course, plans must be submitted and approved by city government and county commissioners. But the most rigorous scrutiny is reserved not for the building but for those involved in owning and managing the casino. These people are vetted by the Nevada Gaming Commission and subjected to a thorough background check.

8 Canyon Ranch Spa + Fitness

The Venetian's spa has an indoor rock climbing wall, two fitness centers, and more than 80 treatment rooms.

5 Nightlife

Spearheaded by the ultra-lavish TAO Nightclub *(see p62)*, along with several resident shows and seven bars and lounges, the Venetian ranks among the Strip's premier nightspots.

9 Casino

Set in the Doge's Palace, the vast casino has 225 table games and 2,000 slot machines. The High-Limit Slots Salon has four parlors, each with slot machines, a sofa, a large TV, and a sound system that allows guests to customize their choice of music. There is a 10,000-sq-ft (929-sq-m) race and sports book on the casino floor, with personal betting stations.

NEED TO KNOW

MAP P2 ■ 3355 Las Vegas Blvd S.
■ 702 414 1000, 877 659 9643 ■ www.
venetian.com ■ $$$ suites only *(for price categories see p84)*

....

■ Splurge on a meal at Emeril Lagasse's Delmonico Steakhouse, or at Wolfgang Puck's lavish restaurant.

■ It is almost as much fun – and a lot less expensive – to watch the gondoliers from land as it is to actually ride in the gondolas.

■ If possible, visit The Venetian when there is a full moon and the crowds have thinned: by moonlight it is breathtaking.

10 Madame Tussauds

In a building fashioned after the library on St. Marks Square, Madame Tussauds *(see p39)* opened here in 1999 and features statues of well-known celebrities such as Marilyn Monroe **(left)**. Some say the waxworks here are even more lifelike than those in the London original.

TOP 10 ⭐ Wynn Las Vegas

Built on the site of the legendary Desert Inn – once owned by billionaire Howard Hughes – this mega-resort was designed to captivate the highest of the high-rollers and the biggest of the big spenders. Over-the-top opulence, from its extravagant villas to exquisite resorts and pools, reigns supreme. Wynn's sister hotel, Encore, is a luxurious addition to the resort, with its own selection of entertainment, restaurants, suites, and shops. The grounds, with an artificial mountain and lake, are spectacular, too.

1 Live Shows
While the Wynn no longer has a resident production show, it does bring in changing major headliners. Legendary musical acts and popular comedians who guest star here include Jim Gaffigan, Bryan Adams, Brad Paisley, Chris Isaak, Trevor Noah, and Demetri Martin. The performances are held in the Encore Theater with its state-of-the art acoustics.

2 Fine Dining
Celebrity restaurants abound at both Wynn and Encore. SW, Wynn's signature steakhouse, is helmed by the innovative chef Mark LoRusso. While the Mizumi restaurant offers the freshest Japanese cuisine. Wing Lei specializes in serving Chinese flavors with western techniques.

3 Casinos
Both the Encore and Wynn casinos seem more intimate than their size would indicate. The gambling stakes are higher than at other casinos, and the casino bars are classy. The decor is lavish, and there's not a flashing light or neon sign in sight. Tile walkways **(right)** provide natural light and views over the indoor oases.

4 Golf Course
Steve Wynn and golfer Tom Fazio collaborated in redesigning this huge course **(left)** by moving tons of desert sand, repositioning trees, and adding features including the waterfall that players walk under to get from the 18th hole to the traditional-style clubhouse.

5 XS
This nightclub at Encore is one of the most impressive in the country. Designed to mirror the curves of the human body, it has an undulating golden staircase at the entrance, top-of-the-line production elements, and pyrotechnics. Bottle service is offered on the dance floor and in the poolside cabanas.

6 Lake of Dreams
Best viewed from the main staircase inside the casino, the extraordinary Lake of Dreams **(below)** is a surreal sound-and-light show in which ethereal illuminated figures emerge from a mist-shrouded lake.

7 The Wynn Esplanade

Behind the glass facades of Cartier, Louis Vuitton, Prada, and almost two dozen other upscale stores, lies temptation galore for big winners. Window shoppers can admire the designs and merchandise present at the Esplanade (left).

ON THE STRIP

The casino magnate and billionaire Steve Wynn opened the Mirage in 1989, starting an era that impacted gaming all around the world. When he unveiled the Bellagio hotel nine years later, the mega-resort trend was born. He described, the Wynn Las Vegas, as "the most expensive, the most complex, the most ambitious structure ever built in the world …" In 2018, Wynn had to step down as chairman of Wynn Resorts owing to accusations of sexual misconduct.

8 Wedding Salons

For visitors planning to marry here, there are two wedding chapels, the Lavender Salon and the Lilac Salon, with private foyers and bridal rooms. The Primrose Court provides a setting for outdoor weddings under a canopy of trees.

9 Spas

Hotel guests can indulge in a range of wraps, massages, and other treatments. Clients can enjoy them in one of the 45 tranquil treatment rooms, or at the poolside cabana.

NEED TO KNOW

MAP N2 ▪ 3131 Las Vegas Blvd S. ▪ 702 770 7000, 888 320 7123 (toll free) ▪ www.wynnlasvegas.com ▪ $$$ (for price categories see p86)

▪ The Buffet features everything from sushi to steak, and is renowned as the finest of the city's "gourmet buffets." There are 16 food kitchens, and the atmosphere is garden-like with topiaries and pretty foliage. Prices vary depending on the time of visit.

▪ Wear walking shoes if you want to explore the resort as there is a lot of ground to cover.

▪ Moderately priced fare can be found at Wynn's dining outlets, including The Cafe and Terrace Pointe Café. Vegan and vegetarian menus available.

10 Encore Beach Club

Epitomizing Las Vegas's new breed of summer-only, pool-party-themed "day-clubs", the opulent 60,000-sq-ft Encore Beach Club (right) attracts world-famous celebrities, such as Paris Hilton.

⭐ The Forum Shops at Caesars Palace

"So many shops and so little time" is the complaint of most first-time visitors to The Forum Shops. Antiquities, celebrity memorabilia, couturier clothes, and art galleries – there are more than 160 stores and restaurants in all. The common areas of the complex are open 24 hours a day, so the savvy visitors who want to window shop and get a close-up view of the fountains and buildings will stroll its lanes in the small hours of the morning.

2 Spiral Escalator

The Forum Shops is home to an impressive freestanding spiral escalator (**left**). At three stories high, it is the first of its kind in the United States. It was designed exclusively for the shopping mall by Mitsubishi and added in 2004 after an expansion to the complex.

3 Sky Ceiling

The domed ceiling simulates a constantly changing sky. The morning sun shines; afternoon clouds float by; evening stars twinkle.

1 Fine Dining

Credited for hosting the Strip's first true fine-dining restaurant, the Forum is now home to Smoked Burgers & BBQ; seafood specialists Water Grill; legendary steakhouse, the Palm; Joe's Seafood, Prime Steak & Stone Crab; Carmine's Italian Restaurant; Sushi Roku, a Strip-view sushi bar on Level 3; and several Italian offerings, including Il Molino of New York.

4 Sports Goods

As well as kit for all US team sports, the enormous, multi-level Nike Store at the Atlantis end of the Forum Shops sells replica gear from the big European soccer teams. If you prefer a more classic look, opt instead for a tennis shirt from Lacoste.

6 Architecture

An ancient Roman Forum streetscape is the inspiration behind the design (**above**). The Roman Great Hall is 160 ft (49 m) in diameter and 85 ft (26 m) high. Look for ornate fountains and classic statuary in the central piazzas, and the 50,000-gallon (189,000-liter) saltwater aquarium.

Men's Fashion 5

Many big-name international menswear brands such as Gucci and Salvatore Ferragamo have stores here (**right**). In addition, Tommy Bahama's sells contemporary resort wear, while both Burberry and John Varvatos cater to a more exclusive clientele.

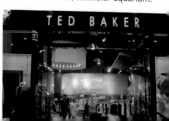

⑦ Women's Fashion

If there's one field in which the mall truly excels, it's women's fashion. There is a range of stores for you to splurge at, from Michael Kor's designer boutique to high-street staples such as Guess, Coach, and H&M **(left)**.

⑧ Casual Dining

As well as more formal restaurants, there are plenty of places to pause for a quick meal. The two main casual restaurants are huge outlets of The Cheesecake Factory and Planet Hollywood. For a pick-me-up, stop off for an espresso at Ciao Ciao.

⑨ Aquarium

Adjacent to the free, animatronic Atlantis Show, which features pyrotechnic effects, and inside the Forum Shops is the Atlantis Aquarium. More than 150 unique species of tropical fish life can be found in the massive 50,000-gallon saltwater aquarium.

Shoes ⑩

Almost 20 stores are devoted to footwear here. Options range from chic Italian shops specializing in luxury women's shoes, such as Valentino and Mephisto, to the Western-wear emporium Kemo Sabe – the place for hand-tooled cowboy boots **(right)**.

COMMERCE OR ENTERTAINMENT?

In most US cities, shopping is an end in itself: go to the mall, make purchases, return home. In Las Vegas, however, shopping has the added dimension of being coupled with entertainment. The Forum Shops and some of the city's other hotels, including Paris Las Vegas and The Venetian, have mimes, musicians, singers, and other performers strolling along the shopping arcades entertaining the crowds. It is all free and adds to the glamour and excitement of Vegas shopping (see pp72–3).

NEED TO KNOW

MAP P1–2 ■ Caesars Palace, 3500 Las Vegas Blvd S. ■ 800 634 6001 ■ Dining reservations: 702 893 4800 ■ www.caesars.com

Shops: open 10am–9pm Sun–Thu (to 10pm Fri & Sat)

■ Have lunch at one of the restaurants with a sidewalk café, from where you can watch the passing parades.

■ Plan your visit during the holiday season to admire the elaborate decorations.

■ If you're visiting with youngsters, arrive early in the morning to avoid the daily rush of shoppers.

■ Walking from the parking garage to the shops is a shorter trek than through the enormous casino.

TOP 10 ⭐ Downtown Las Vegas

During the 1980s and early 1990s, as the Strip became ever more glamorous, the Downtown area – including the stretch along Fremont Street, formerly known as Glitter Gulch – went further into decline. City fathers and casino owners agreed that something had to be done to reverse the process and took action to see that it was. The resulting efforts have revitalized the area. Development is ongoing, with the opening of new restaurants and attractions offering a greater range of entertainment.

3 Fremont Street Experience

Running from Main St to Fourth St, Fremont Street's *(see p91)* most prominent feature is Viva Vision, located near the Plaza Hotel-Casino **(right)**. This is the world's largest graphic display system, containing more than 12.5 million LED lights, which provides spectacular nightly light-and-sound shows every hour from dusk until midnight.

1 Neon Lights

Downtown is home to the city's classic neon lights and signs **(above)**. This is one of the brightest places on earth – so much so that you can stand on the street at midnight and read a newspaper. Even before the Fremont Street Experience was conceived, the country's leading neon designers and engineers were displaying their talent here.

4 Signs of the Past

Vegas Vic *(see p92)* has been waving to passers-by on Fremont Street since 1951. More illuminating insights into the history of neon can be found at the Neon Museum *(see p91)* at 770 N. Las Vegas Blvd.

2 Las Vegas's First Casino

The place where it all started is the Sal Sagev Hotel on Fremont Street, now the Golden Gate. Considered Las Vegas's most historic boutique hotel and casino, the original, strange-looking name makes sense in mirror-writing.

5 Binion's

Dallas bootlegger and gambler Benny Binion established the property **(left)** in 1951, and it was owned until 2004 by his descendants. The biggest names in poker continue to play here, although the World Series of Poker has moved to Rio *(see p100)*. The hotel-casino is worth a visit to appreciate its old-time atmosphere.

6 SlotZilla Zip Line

The 12-story SlotZilla **(left)** is the launch point for two separate zip lines, on which riders can either zoom above the crowds sitting up, or fly face-first like Superman.

7 Fremont Street Pedestrian Promenade

There is direct access to ten casinos and more than 60 restaurants from the promenade. Enjoy the vibe of open casinos, where the action spills out onto the streets.

8 Downtown Container Park

Housed in converted shipping containers, this open-air shopping center, on 707 Fremont Street, has boutique shops, bars, restaurants, and galleries. The center also hosts live entertainment and in the 4K visual Dome planetarium, there are immersive 360-degree, ultra-HD videos as well.

9 Entertainment

In addition to the production shows and lounge acts at most of the hotels, Fremont Street is a center of entertainment and a popular venue for parades and musical performances.

10 Golden Nugget

The four-star Golden Nugget **(right)** is the best-value hotel in the city (rates can fall as low as $59 in the off-season). Its casino is also first-rate *(see p55)*. Dine at the Chart House for its ambience – and also for a great view of the huge aquarium.

BEGINNINGS

For almost 20 years after its incorporation, entertainment in Las Vegas was limited to a few bars and brothels in the red-light district Downtown. The legalization of gambling and arrival of as many as 5,000 dam construction workers in 1931 changed all that. Casinos opened on Fremont Street, and tourists began to arrive. World War II personnel and their families gave Las Vegas another population surge in the 1940s, and casino building continued apace after the war – as it does to this day.

NEED TO KNOW

MAP J–L4, L3

Golden Gate: 1 Fremont St; 702 385 1906

Golden Nugget: 129 Fremont St; 702 385 7111

Binion's: 128 Fremont St; 702 382 1600

SlotZilla Zip Line: 425 Fremont St; 702 678 5780

■ For tasty American fare served alongside outstanding cocktails, try Therapy *(518 Fremont St)*.

■ Most of the action at night in Downtown Las Vegas takes place near the Fremont Street Experience.

■ Arrive a few minutes before the hour to see the show at the Fremont Street Experience. Then explore the shops and casinos, or enjoy the stage entertainment.

TOP 10 ⭐ CityCenter

Las Vegas's largest creation is CityCenter, a "city-within-a-city" designed to have everything in one place. Located on 67 acres (27 ha) at the heart of the Strip, the complex is home to five distinct properties – ARIA Resort, The Shops at Crystals, the Waldorf Astoria, the Vdara Hotel, and the residential Veer Towers. The area also contains a casino, luxury spas, and shops, all within a short distance of each other. At a cost of $8.5 billion, CityCenter is the most expensive privately funded project in the United States.

Architecture ①
Unique architectural features by eight of the world's foremost architects, including Cesar Pelli, abound at CityCenter. Among the highlights is Crystals' quartz-shaped metal-and-glass exterior by Studio Daniel Libeskind (right).

② The Park
Nestled between the Park MGM and New York-New York resorts, this dining and entertainment district is a short walk away from CityCenter. There are six restaurants and a T-Mobile Arena, where concerts and sporting events – including home games of the Vegas Golden Knights NHL hockey team – are held.

③ ARIA Express
The sleek, free cable-drawn tram (above) that connects the ARIA Resort with the Monte Carlo to the south and Bellagio to the north is an exhilarating vision, straight from some futuristic cityscape. A journey offers an interesting vantage point of CityCenter.

NEED TO KNOW

MAP Q1–2 ▪ 3740 Las Vegas Blvd S.

ARIA Resort and Casino: 3730 Las Vegas Blvd S.; 866 359 7111; $$

The Shops at Crystals: 3720 Las Vegas Blvd S.; 702 590 9202

Waldorf Astoria: 3752 Las Vegas Blvd S.; 702 590 8888; $$

Vdara Hotel: 2600 W. Harmon Ave; 866 745 7111; $$

▪ Head to Starbucks to start your day with a coffee and a breakfast sandwich, on the mezzanine level of Crystals, near the main entrance by ARIA Resort and Casino.

▪ The ARIA Express links CityCenter, Bellagio and Park MGM in 3 minutes.

For a key to hotel price ranges see p86

④ Fine Art Collection

There are great permanent displays of fine art throughout CityCenter. Artists such as Maya Lin, Jenny Holzer, Frank Stella, and Richard Long have created pieces ranging from sculptures and paintings to large-scale indoor and outdoor installations.

ECO-FRIENDLY SITE

CityCenter was built with sustainability in mind, and the project has been certified by the US Green Building Council. The ARIA is one of the largest hotels in the world with Leadership in Energy and Environmental Design (LEED) status. Features include natural lighting, an on-site combined heat and power plant, and an extensive recycling program.

⑦ The Shops at Crystals

Shopping, dining, and entertainment are all found under one roof at this vast retail center. More than 50 designer stores include Tom Ford, Versace, and the largest Louis Vuitton boutique in North America. Various works of art, including a three-story, nest-like Tree House **(above)** and ice and water sculptures, are dotted throughout.

⑧ Dining

Mastro's Ocean Club is a top dining place known for its signature three-tiered iced seafood tower and succulent bone-in fillet.

⑨ Vdara Hotel

This 57-story, all-suite hotel and spa **(below)** connects to the Bellagio *(see pp14–15)* and the ARIA via a walkway. Suites boast state-of-the-art technology and full-service kitchens.

⑤ Spas

CityCenter spas include the ARIA, with a water garden; the Vdara, offering holistic treatments; and the chic Waldorf Astoria with a surfeit of marble and gold.

⑥ ARIA Resort and Casino

The ARIA Resort and Casino **(below)** boasts 4,004 high-tech guest rooms and suites with views of the skyline and surrounding mountains. There are four outdoor pools, 15 restaurants, 7 bars, a spa, and a theater *(see p86)*.

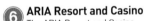

⑩ Waldorf Astoria

Winner of the Forbes Five-Star Award in its former guise as the Mandarin Oriental, the stylish Waldorf Astoria is a 47-story, non-gaming hotel with 389 rooms and suites, and 225 luxury condominiums. Guests check in at the Sky Lobby, and there is a sky bridge to Crystals at CityCenter.

TOP 10 ⭐ Hoover Dam and Lake Mead

Before the construction of the Hoover Dam early last century, the mighty Colorado River often flooded farmland in southern California and Mexico. A series of studies into how to tame the rampaging river led in 1928 to the Boulder Canyon Project Act and the subsequent construction of the dam. This colossus of concrete – a triumph of engineering – not only provides reliable water supplies, flood control, and electricity, but is also a huge tourist attraction, with nearly a million visitors per year.

1 Hoover Dam Visitor Center

Audiovisual and theater presentations as well as multimedia exhibits at the Visitor Center **(below)** explain the processes and perils involved in building this eighth wonder of the modern world. An over-look on top of the center provides a bird's-eye view of the dam, Lake Mead, the Hoover Dam Bridge, and the Black Canyon.

4 Hoover Dam Bridge

Get an unrivaled view of the dam from the Hoover Dam Bridge also known as the Mike O'Callaghan–Pat Tillman Memorial Bridge **(right)**. Inaugurated in 2010, the sight of 3.2 million cubic yards (2.6 million cubic m) of concrete, standing 727 ft (221 m) high, is truly awe-inspiring.

5 Commercial District, Boulder City

Walk back into 1930s America. The arcaded buildings were the precursors of today's shopping plazas. Boulder Dam Hotel, by contrast, is in Dutch colonial style.

6 Lake Mead Cruises

The lake's shores come to life seen from the deck of a boat **(below)**. You'll see sandy beaches and rocks of every hue. Look out for burros, jack-rabbits, lizards, and bighorn sheep, too.

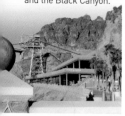

2 Construction Workers' Houses, Boulder City

Up to 8,000 dam workers were housed here, and although many of the buildings have disappeared, cottages 1–12 look much as they did when first built.

3 Lake Mead

The dam's lake is the largest artificial body of water in the US. Its 550 miles (885 km) of shoreline boasts canyons and flower-rich meadows; its waters abound with fish. Boulder Beach offers the best swimming.

Tours of the Powerplant and the Dam 7

Visitors can descend 530 ft (162 m) for a power-plant tour, or explore the dam's tunnels **(right)**.

Scuba Diving 8

An extraordinary underwater scene greets divers: in addition to fish, there is a submerged factory where trainloads of gravel for the dam's concrete were cleaned and sorted. Take a trip with a local company; certified divers can rent scuba gear.

Hoover Dam Museum, Boulder City 9

The dam and the people who built it are the focus of this museum, which is housed in the historic Boulder Dam Hotel *(see p105)*. Don't forget to watch the film chronicling the construction of the dam. Memorabilia, photos, and posters give more insights into life in 1930s US.

ANCIENT PEOPLES

Archaeologists disagree about how long humans have lived in the desert along the Colorado River. There were certainly people living downstream from the dam 3,000–4,000 years ago, maybe as far back as 8,000 years ago. The Patayans were among the first Native American peoples known to live in the broader tri-state area (Nevada, Arizona, California), appearing in about AD 900. They lived in brush shelters and ate seeds and plants. The Hualapai and Mojave peoples are said to be the descendents of the Patayans.

NEED TO KNOW

MAP T2 ■ 30 miles (50 km) SE of Las Vegas ■ www.usbr.gov/lc/hooverdam

Hoover Dam Visitor Center: Hwy 93, Hoover Dam, Boulder City, NV; 702 494 2517; open 9am–4:15pm daily

Tour reservations: 866 730 9097 (toll free)

■ While driving through Boulder City, stock up on a light meal at Capriotti's Sandwich Shop *(1010 Nevada Highway)* to have it later on a Lake Mead beach.

■ Take a cruise that does not include meals: it will be cheaper and gives you more time to take in the surroundings.

■ Drive along the west shore of Lake Mead to access the Valley of Fire and Lost City Museum *(see p111)*.

Black Canyon River Raft Trips 10

The Colorado River flows lazily below the dam, so rafting **(above)** is pleasant rather than white-knuckle. It takes a little more than 3 hours to make the 12-mile (19-km) trip to Willow Beach. Look out for petroglyphs carved in the rock, and for ringbolts: before the dam existed, these were used to winch steamboats through Ringbolt Rapids.

TOP 10 ⭐ Red Rock Canyon

About 225 million years ago, everything at Red Rock Canyon was covered by an inland sea. The escarpment, formations, and caves were created after that sea evaporated, and wind and rain began sculpting the land. This remarkable desert region lies just 24 miles (39 km) from the middle of the Strip. A conservation area since 1990, it is protected from city expansion. The 13-mile (21-km) scenic drive that loops off Highway 159 provides a good overview, but the best way to explore this part of the Mojave Desert is on foot.

Red Rock Vista Overlook ③

The view (right) from this overlook, about 1 mile (1.5 km) past the Highway 159 turnoff to the Canyon, is of the Red Rock escarpment, which rises a breathtaking 3,000 ft (1,000 m) from the valley floor. Time your trip to get here at sunrise or sunset when the colors of the sandstone are at their best.

① Hikes and Guided Walks

Of more than 30 miles (50 km) of hiking trails in the canyon (above), the most popular include those to Calico Tanks (featuring red sandstone) and Oak Creek. Guided walks focus on aspects of the environment such as native wildflowers and the area's geology.

② Endangered Desert Tortoises

Look out for brown-shelled tortoises, which, with their lifespan of up to 100 years, may outlive you. They dig burrows in the desert and spend at least 95 per cent of their long lives below ground. Astonishingly, adult tortoises can survive for a year without water.

④ Children's Discovery Trail

At the visitor center, inquire about the *Junior Ranger Discovery Book* and scheduled educational events. Near Willow Springs is the Children's Discovery Trail to Lost Creek. Less than 1 mile (1.5 km) long, it highlights points of interest on the way. The cliffs above it are a good place to spot bighorn sheep.

⑤ Visitor Center

The visitor center (below) has area maps, and staff on hand to answer questions. It contains both indoor and outdoor exhibits featuring geological, cultural, and natural history displays.

⑥ Bookstore

The visitor center bookstore covers the local flora, fauna, and geology. Excellent Southwest-themed novels for children and books on local geology, history, and culture are available for purchase.

7 Petroglyphs and Pictographs

The area around Willow Springs contains some fascinating prehistoric rock carvings and paintings **(left)**. The exact meaning of many of the incised and painted symbols is not known, but because the area's early inhabitants were hunters and gatherers, it is believed that many symbolize the procuring of food.

8 Thirteen-Mile Drive

The main scenic loop is a road taking in the Calico Hills, and Rainbow and Bridge mountains. There are stopping points for views along it. Head for Willow Springs for picnics. Most hiking trails are accessible from parking lots on the loop.

9 Tinajas

Prevalent in the Calico Hills and at White Rock Spring, tinajas (or tanks) are naturally formed rock catchments for water. They serve as drinking basins for wildlife and are good places to seek out for photo opportunities.

10 Desert Whiptail Lizards

Common to the western US, these lizards **(below)** have pointed snouts and forked tongues. Recognize them by the four or five light stripes along the back, and the yellow- or cream-colored belly with scattered dark spots.

CYCLING CULTURE

Highway 159, which leads out of Las Vegas toward Red Rock Canyon, is very popular with cyclists, especially on weekend mornings. Use caution when driving on this road. Visitors who want to ride can rent bikes at Las Vegas Cyclery (10575 Discovery Dr), Trek Bicycle (4305 S. Fort Apache Rd), and other businesses. Keep an eye out for desert creatures such as jackrabbits and snakes that may dart out onto the road. Take plenty of water and sunscreen.

NEED TO KNOW

MAP T2 ■ 24 miles (38 km) from mid-Strip

Adm: $15 per vehicle plus $2 reservation fee; campground: $15 per night, per site; www.recreation.gov/timed-entry/10075177

Visitor Center: 1000 Scenic Dr; 702 515 5350; open 9am–4:30pm daily; www.redrockcanyonlv.org

■ Stop at a deli or takeout in Las Vegas to pick up a picnic lunch to eat at the Willow Springs picnic area.

■ Wheelchair users will find plenty of accessible sights to explore near the visitor center and Red Spring boardwalk.

■ You will need a permit to camp overnight or go rock-climbing at Red Rock Canyon. Apply at the visitor center.

■ Take the usual precautions when visiting a desert area (see p128).

TOP 10 ⭐ Grand Canyon

"Overwhelming" and "humbling" are words frequently used to describe the Grand Canyon experience. One of the world's most awesome sights, the canyon is 277 miles (446 km) long, 10 miles (16 km) wide, and as deep as a mile (1.6 km) in places. The canyon encompasses a range of desert and mountain habitats. Day-trippers from Las Vegas usually fly to Grand Canyon West. The more impressive South and North rims lie in the national park, a five-hour drive from the city; best seen with an overnight stay.

Skywalk **1**

Jutting out above a fearsome 4,000-ft (1,200-m) abyss at the canyon's less dramatic western end, the horseshoe-shaped, glass-floored Skywalk is the highlight of a day-trip to the Grand Canyon West. You can't take your own camera with you, but don't worry – it's not an experience you're likely to forget **(right)**.

2 Flyovers

Flights over Grand Canyon **(below)** make for popular day trips (see p119) from Las Vegas.

4 Visitor Centers

Information centers at the North and South Rims of the canyon supply free maps as well as *The Guide*, which has general park information; *The Junior Ranger Guide*, listing children's activities; and *The Accessibility Guide*, which has information for differently abled visitors. Exhibits and bookstores are located near these centers, as are great observation points too. Ask about evening ranger programs if you plan on spending the night in the park.

3 Tusayan Ruins and Museum

Ruins of rock dwellings inhabited by ancestors of the Hopi peoples around AD 1200 are preserved between South Rim Village and the park's east entrance. The museum has artifacts and exhibits offering an insight into their culture.

5 Whitewater Rafting

Many companies, such as Canyon Explorations (see p119), offer white-water rafting trips **(right)** along the Colorado River on the canyon floor. Trips vary in length from 6 to 16 days.

⑥ Grand Canyon Railway

Vintage train services **(right)** connect Williams to the Grand Canyon's South Rim year-round. From February to October, a steam locomotive is used monthly.

THE INDIGENOUS PEOPLES OF THE CANYON

The Grand Canyon was home to the Ancestral Puebloan people for thousands of years. With the arrival of settlers seeking land and gold in the mid-1800s, the Indigenous peoples were relocated to reservations, after several years of warfare with the colonizers. Today, several tribes still live on reservations in the area, including the Havasupai, Hualapai, Navajo, and Hopi.

⑦ Overlooks

Grand views may be found from many canyon overlooks. On the South Rim, Hermit Road hugs the rim west of Grand Canyon Village with nine overlooks. Enjoy great views of the Colorado River far below from Pima Point. Motorists can use Desert View Drive (Hwy 64) along the South Rim east of Grand Canyon Village with spectacular views from Grandview and Moran points, and you can almost see down to Utah from the top of the 70-ft (21-m) Watchtower.

⑧ Hiking Trails

Popular South Rim hikes are the South Kaibab, Bright Angel, and Rim trails *(see p118)*. North Rim hikes include the North Kaibab, Bright Angel Point, and Widforss trails. Don't hike to the canyon floor and back in one day: get an overnight permit.

NEED TO KNOW

MAP V2 ■ South Rim 271 miles (436 km), North Rim 255 miles (408 km) E. of Las Vegas

Visitor Center: 928 638 7888; open 9am–4pm daily (hours vary in summer); adm national park \$35 per vehicle or \$20 per pedestrian or cyclist; www.nps.gov/grca

■ There are some great places to eat *(see p120)* at the Grand Canyon.

■ The South Rim is accessible by road year-round, but the North Rim facilities and road are closed from mid-Oct or Nov to mid-May.

■ You will need a permit to camp outside the official campsites within the national park. Apply in advance at the Backcountry Information Center *(www.nps.gov/grca/planyourvisit)*.

⑨ California Condors

Standing over 3 ft (1 m) tall and with a wingspan of about 9 ft (3 m), the rare California condor may be spotted flying over the South Rim in summer.

⑩ Grand Canyon West

Grand Canyon West **(above)** is on the Hualapai Reservation near Lake Mead. As well as the Skywalk, it has other viewpoints and themed attractions for guests to enjoy.

Following pages Viewpoint over the Grand Canyon

The Top 10
of Everything

**Luminous casino sign
on Fremont Street**

TOP10 Moments in History

The neon sign outside the Flamingo Hotel and Casino

① 1855: Mormons Establish a Trading Post

Inhabited for centuries by Southern Paiute peoples and encountered by Spanish explorers in 1829, the Las Vegas area was settled in 1855 by a group of Mormons, led by Brigham Young, who established a trading post here.

② 1860s: Paiute Peoples are Dispossessed

After the settlement expanded, much of the Southern Paiute land was taken up by the railroad. Some 10 acres (4 ha) of Downtown Las Vegas land was deeded to the Paiute peoples in 1911, creating the Las Vegas Colony. In 1983, the Congress returned to them about 3,800 acres (1,537 ha) of land, now known as the Snow Mountain Reservation of the Las Vegas Paiute Tribe.

③ 1931: Gambling Legalized in Nevada

The relaxed gaming laws passed in the Silver State in 1931 encouraged widespread public participation in betting and gambling, though both had already been widely popular.

④ 1940s: Air Conditioning and Irrigation Arrive

The ability of air conditioning and irrigation to keep buildings cool and land green attracted developers to the Nevada desert. In 1941, hotelier Tom Hull bought land 3 miles (5 km) south of Downtown for $150 an acre and built the El Rancho motel – a new concept in accommodation.

⑤ 1946, Christmas Day: Bugsy Siegel Opens the Flamingo Hotel and Casino

A handful of hotels and motels followed El Rancho, but only when mobster Benjamin "Bugsy" Siegel built the Flamingo Hotel and Casino did the town adopt the Miami Beach-style feel – the hallmark of the Strip.

⑥ 1960: The Rat Pack Comes to Town

The Flamingo was widely imitated in the 1950s, and entertainment was an important part of its allure. Frank Sinatra performed at the Sands Hotel in 1960, and after that Las Vegas became a playground of the so-called Rat Pack (Sinatra, Sammy Davis, Jr., Dean Martin, Peter Lawford, et al).

The Rat Pack

7 1966: Howard Hughes Arrives

Howard Hughes's Summa Corporation was a dominant player in the Nevada hotel/casino industry. Legend (which makes up much of Las Vegas's history) has it that the eccentric billionaire arrived in town one day in 1966 by limousine and was whisked up to his suite at the Desert Inn, where he lived as a recluse for several years, with uncut fingernails and hair.

Eccentric billionaire Howard Hughes

8 1990s: The Era of the Theme Hotel Begins

In the 1970s and 1980s, Las Vegas hotels became larger and more flamboyant. In 1991, the ground-breaking luxury hotels MGM Grand, Treasure Island, and pyramid-shaped Luxor were launched, promoting the theme hotel concept in earnest.

9 1998: Bellagio Opens

The luxurious Bellagio (see pp14–15) set a new standard for Las Vegas hotels. Its founder is acknowledged as the creative force behind the modern resort concept.

10 2009 Onwards: The Next Generation

Las Vegas' economic standing proved its resilience to recession with the unveiling of the futuristic CityCenter neighborhood in 2009. In a similar fashion, in 2019, the city saw the construction of the 65,000-seat Allegiant Stadium, broke ground on the 18,000-seat MGS Sphere arena, and in 2021, opened the Resorts World Las Vegas resort.

TOP 10 FAMOUS RESIDENTS

1 Phyllis McGuire
The entertainer is fondly remembered as one third of the singing McGuire Sisters, whose hits included "Sincerely."

2 Jerry Lewis
The comedian who famously teamed up with singer Dean Martin performed in Las Vegas for many years.

3 Howard Hughes
The eccentric billionaire used his inheritance to make still more money in the film and airline industries before becoming a force in gambling.

4 Liberace
Wladziu Valentino Liberace – aka "Mr. Show Business" – first opened at the legendary (now closed) Riviera in 1955.

5 Wayne Newton
In 1957, entertainer Wayne Newton started his career at the Fremont casino; he still frequents events in the city.

6 Steffi Graf and Andre Agassi
The top tennis stars have lived in Las Vegas since they got married in 2001.

7 Debbie Reynolds
The film star was also the owner of a hotel-casino and a museum displaying Hollywood memorabilia.

8 Carlos Santana
The Mexican-born guitar maestro famous for fusing rock 'n' roll with latin jazz is a resident of Las Vegas.

9 Mike Tyson
Former world heavyweight champion Mike Tyson has lived in Henderson, Las Vegas, since 2008.

10 Clara Bow
Silent-film star Clara Bow, who became known as the "It Girl," lived in Las Vegas with her actor husband Rex Bell.

Silent-film star Clara Bow

TOP 10 Museums and Galleries

1 Luxor Exhibits

MAP R1 ■ Luxor, 3900 Las Vegas Blvd S. ■ 702 262 4400 ■ Open 11am–6pm daily ■ Adm ■ www.titaniclasvegas.com; www.bodiestheexhibition.com

The Luxor pyramid's upper level holds two fascinating permanent displays. *Titanic: The Artifact Exhibition* tells the story of the ill-fated liner, and preserves items recovered from the wreck, while *Bodies: The Exhibition* is a gruesome but gripping gallery of plastinated human corpses.

2 Atomic Testing Museum

MAP Q4 ■ 755 E. Flamingo Rd ■ 702 794 5151 ■ Open 9:30am–3:30pm Thu–Tue ■ Adm ■ www.nationalatomictestingmuseum.org

Nevada was the leading nuclear-testing facility in the US from 1951 to 1992, and this museum tells the history of the Atomic Era with artifacts and recreations from the Cold War period. The Ground Zero Theater is a bunker replica that shows visitors a film of an atomic explosion, accompanied by sounds, hot air, and vibrations. Las Vegas's weather station is located outside.

3 Nevada State Museum and Historical Society

MAP C3 ■ 333 S. Valley View Blvd, at the Springs Preserve ■ 702 822 7700 ■ Open 9am–4pm Fri–Mon ■ Adm ■ www.springspreserve.org

This museum has a collection that includes specimens from Nevada mines, preserved Nevada wildlife, Las Vegas showgirl costumes, and a $25,000 chip from the Dunes hotel.

4 Las Vegas Natural History Museum

MAP J5 ■ 900 Las Vegas Blvd N. ■ 702 384 3466 ■ Open 9am–4pm daily ■ Adm ■ www.lvnhm.org

Highlights include the international wildlife room, a children's hands-on exploration room, and a marine-life gallery. The Treasures of Egypt exhibit features reproduced artifacts of ancient Egyptian life.

Dinosaur, Natural History Museum

5 Bellagio Gallery of Fine Art

MAP Q1–2 ■ Bellagio, 3600 Las Vegas Blvd S. ■ 702 693 7871 ■ Open 10am–6:30pm daily ■ Adm ■ www.bellagio.com

This world-class gallery presents temporary exhibitions of 19th- and 20th-century artworks and objects drawn from international collections.

Displays at The Mob Museum

6 The Mob Museum

MAP J4 ▪ 307 Stewart Ave ▪ 702 229 2734 ▪ Open 9am–9pm daily ▪ Adm ▪ www.themob museum.org

Set in the Downtown courthouse that once hosted Senate hearings into organized crime, this lively, exhaustive museum traces the decades-long entanglement between Las Vegas and mobsters, gangsters, and G-men. There is also an adults only speakeasy bar and distillery.

7 Clark County Museum

MAP G6 ▪ 1830 S. Boulder Hwy, Henderson ▪ 702 455 7955 ▪ Open 9am–4:30pm daily ▪ Adm

This unusual museum showcases historic buildings that have been relocated from around the state, as well as contemporary local artifacts.

8 Las Vegas Springs Preserve

MAP C3 ▪ 333 S. Valley View Blvd ▪ 702 822 7700 ▪ Open 9am–4pm Fri–Mon ▪ Adm ▪ www.springspreserve.org

The Springs Preserve explores the history of Las Vegas through exhibits, botanical gardens, hiking trails, animal shows, galleries, classes, and events for the whole family.

9 The Neon Museum

MAP D2–3 ▪ 770 Las Vegas Blvd N. ▪ 702 387 6366 ▪ Tours: 3–11pm daily (2–10pm during winter) – call or book on website ▪ Adm ▪ www.neonmuseum.org

Here, neon signs are considered a form of art. The museum has on display a fascinating and eclectic collection of outdoor signage that casts an illuminating glow on Las Vegas history. The signs date from the 1930s to the present day.

10 Madame Tussauds

MAP P2 ▪ The Venetian, 3377 Las Vegas Blvd S. ▪ 702 862 7800 ▪ Open 11am–7pm daily ▪ Adm ▪ www.madame tussauds.com/LasVegas

Get up close to your favorite celebrity at this branch of the famous waxwork museum. For authenticity, many items of clothing and props used in the exhibitions have been purchased at celebrity auctions.

Display at The Neon Museum

🔟 Theme Hotels

3 Caesars Palace
MAP P1–2 ▪ 3570 Las Vegas Blvd S. ▪ 866 227 5938 ▪ www.caesarspalace.com ▪ $$

Caesars Palace opened in 1966 and was long the Strip's most opulent and most ostentatious hotel. Fifty years on, Caesars continues to spend millions updating its ancient-Roman theme to keep up with newcomers. The cocktail goddesses still wear toga-like costumes, and Cleopatra's Barge (a floating lounge) is still here too, but the entire Strip frontage has become an open-air plaza, dominated by the vast Colosseum, which plays host to performers like Rod Stewart and Sting.

1 The Venetian
Whether or not The Venetian *(see pp16–17)* actually succeeds in evoking accurate images of Venice is beside the point: all of the hotel's parts come together to create an aesthetically pleasing whole.

2 Luxor
MAP R1 ▪ Luxor Hotel and Casino, 3900 Las Vegas Blvd S. ▪ 702 262 4000 ▪ www.luxor.com ▪ $$

One of the most distinctive buildings on the Strip, Luxor's 30-floor pyramid fronted by a giant sphinx sets the tone of this resort. Inside is a replica of the Great Temple of Ramesses II and tiered stories that lead to the top of the pyramid.

4 Bellagio
Although the elegant Bellagio casino *(see pp14–15)* is modeled on the real-life village of Bellagio, set on the coast of Lake Como in northern Italy, its decor is more generally intended to evoke the *belle époque* opulence of Europe in the years before World War I began. The casino's overall grandeur is designed to surpass legendary European hotels of the era, such as the Ritz Paris. Be sure not to miss seeing the Roman gardens, which are situated just behind the check-in desk.

The porte-cochère in Bellagio

Statue of Liberty, New York–New York

while the vibrant dining and nightlife options attract a trendy crowd. There is also a spa, two swimming pools, and a 6,700-seat theater.

(8) Paris Las Vegas
MAP Q2 ■ 3655 Las Vegas Blvd S. ■ 702 946 7000 ■ www. caesars.com/paris-las-vegas ■ $$

Alas, the City of Light has to lose something in translation to the City of Bright Lights. Even so, the Eiffel Tower model is impressive; the bicycle-riding delivery boy and a cheery *"Bonjour"* from valet-parking attendants are nice touches, too.

(9) Circus Circus
As its name suggests, this hotel-casino *(see p81)* features amazing circus acts (no animals are involved) and an indoor, 5-acre (2-ha) theme park.

(5) New York–New York
MAP R1–2 ■ 3790 Las Vegas Blvd S. ■ 702 740 6969 ■ www.newyorknewyork.com ■ $$

The Statue of Liberty raises her torch over the busiest intersection in Las Vegas. Nearby, the Empire State, CBS, and Chrysler Buildings rub shoulders with the Brooklyn Bridge, Grand Central Station, and the New York Public Library. New York-New York is an exciting place to stay, with all manner of well-observed details throughout.

(6) The Mirage
MAP P1–2 ■ 3400 Las Vegas Blvd S. ■ www.mirage.com

The Mirage mimics the tropical landscape of Polynesia, with a virtual rainforest that includes palm trees; a swimming pool with lush vegetation, and a tall volcano, from which a constant waterfall flows. Behind the reception desk is a huge aquarium, which has more than 1,000 sea creatures.

(7) Planet Hollywood
MAP Q2 ■ 3667 Las Vegas Blvd S. ■ 702 785 5555 ■ www.caesars.com/planet-hollywood ■ $$

Las Vegas goes Hollywood at this stunningly modern resort and casino conveniently located near the center of the Strip. The 2,567 movie-themed rooms will appeal to cinema fans,

Indoor theme park at Circus Circus

(10) Excalibur
MAP R1–2 ■ 3850 Las Vegas Blvd S. ■ 702 597 7777 ■ www.excalibur.com ■ $$

One of the first theme hotels (built in 1990), this is still a favorite, and a big hit with children. The legend of King Arthur and his Knights is the theme that runs through the games arcade and continues into the "Canterbury Wedding Chapel."

For a key to hotel price ranges see p86

ᵀᴼᴾ10 Wedding Chapels

① Viva Las Vegas
MAP L3 ▪ 1205 Las Vegas Blvd S. ▪ 702 384 0771

This chapel is known for its Elvis-themed and traditional weddings, as well as ceremonies set against backdrops such as the Red Rock Canyon. Stars like Angelina Jolie and Matt LeBlanc have made appearances here.

② Bellagio Wedding Chapels
MAP Q1–2 ▪ Bellagio, 3600 Las Vegas Blvd S. ▪ 702 693 7700, 888 464 4436

Bellagio's two chapels provide some of the most elegant and romantic wedding venues in Las Vegas. Both have a stained-glass window behind the altar, while ornate lamps and chandeliers of amethyst and Venetian glass complement the pastel shades of the furnishings. Personalized services are available, as well as both wedding and reception planning.

Elegant wedding chapel at Bellagio

③ Little Church of the West
MAP C5 ▪ 4617 Las Vegas Blvd S. ▪ 702 739 7971

The Little Church of the West opened in 1942, making it the oldest wedding chapel in Las Vegas. It is a favorite with the stars: Zsa Zsa Gabor and George Sanders, Angelina Jolie and Billy Bob Thornton, and Cindy Crawford and Richard Gere have all graced its aisle.

④ Jewish Temples
Temple Beth Sholom (Conservative United), 10700 Havenwood Ln ▪ 702 804 1333

There are very few churches and synagogues – as distinct from wedding chapels – that perform "walk-in" ceremonies. Marriage requirements vary from congregation to congregation. Contact Temple Beth Sholom for further information.

⑤ Christ Church Episcopal
MAP M4 ▪ 2000 S. Maryland Parkway ▪ 702 735 7655

This traditional Episcopal church is the closest one to the Strip. Bear in mind that churches in the Episcopal Diocese of Nevada require couples to attend prenuptial meetings with the rector of the church before a wedding can be performed.

⑥ Chapel of the Flowers
MAP L3 ▪ 1717 Las Vegas Blvd S. ▪ 702 735 4331

Of the three separate chapels in this picturesque little ensemble, the Victorian Chapel is the most popular with couples seeking a touch of tradition. There is also a waterfall and a "glass garden" adorned with illuminated glass flowers.

Indoor wedding salon at Wynn

7 Wedding Salons at Wynn
MAP N2 ■ Wynn Las Vegas, 3131 Las Vegas Blvd S. ■ 702 770 7400

Wynn Las Vegas has three wedding salons to choose from – two are indoors and one is outdoors. For couples hoping to ease the stress off the big day, nine all-inclusive wedding packages are available, ranging from the simple to the over-the-top opulent.

8 The Chapel at Excalibur
MAP R1–2 ■ Excalibur, 3850 Las Vegas Blvd S. ■ 702 597 7278

Create your own version of Camelot by marrying your knight in shining armor in one of Excalibur's two medieval-style chapels. Although Excalibur no longer rents medieval costumes, one can opt for a more contemporary, romantic appeal. There is also the option to have an alfresco service, right in front of the castle. Vow-renewal services are also on offer for the already-wed.

9 Sundance Helicopters
MAP C5 ■ 5596 Haven St ■ 702 736 0606, 800 653 1881

For a truly unforgettable wedding day, Sundance Helicopters offers this all-inclusive package. A stretch limousine whisks you to a private helicopter that carries you to Grand Canyon West for a marriage ceremony overlooking the Colorado River, before flying you back over the Strip.

10 A Little White Wedding Chapel
MAP L4 ■ 1301 Las Vegas Blvd S. ■ 702 382 5943

This wedding chapel represents what for many people is the epitome of Las Vegas; it has acquired a reputation for hosting rather unusual weddings. It was here in the spring of 2001 that a mass wedding took place, officiated by multiple Elvises. And for the bride and groom who are acting on impulse or those who have a hectic schedule, the Little White Wedding Chapel offers a drive-through wedding window, Tunnel of Love, where they can exchange vows without leaving their car. There is also a choice of five indoor chapels, and an outdoor gazebo. The window is open daily from 9am to 9pm, and no appointment is necessary.

The drive-through at A Little White Wedding Chapel

🔟 Golf Courses

location provides stunning panoramic views of the Strip *(see pp12–13)*, and the impressive layout has bunkers, water hazards, rolling terrain, and narrow fairways, which add to the challenge this course offers.

1 Spanish Trail Golf Club
MAP A5 ▪ 5050 Spanish Trail Ln ▪ 702 364 5050

Designed by Robert Trent Jones, Jr., this club offers three individual nines that can be played in three different 18-hole combinations. The 27 holes at the club offer undulating greens and tree-lined fairways. The Lakes Course has water coming into play on six of its nine holes.

2 Highland Falls at Golf Summerlin
10201 Sun City Blvd ▪ 702 254 7010

Former Masters winner Billy Casper designed this course, which reaches an elevation of 3,053 ft (930 m). The

3 DragonRidge Country Club
MAP E6 ▪ 552 S. Stephanie St, Henderson ▪ 702 745 2391

With its manicured fairways, bent-grass greens, and dramatic elevation changes, DragonRidge offers some of the most spectacular views in the valley. The course is private, with limited public play.

4 Angel Park Golf Club
MAP A3 ▪ 100 S. Rampart Blvd ▪ 702 254 4653

The Palm and the Mountain, this club's two 18-hole championship layouts designed by the legendary American golfer Arnold Palmer, have been described by Angel Park as the "world's most complete golf experience," and it's hard to disagree. A night-lighted driving range, a 9-hole putting course, and a golf school also form part of the complex.

Professional Golfer Kevin Na in action at Golf Summerlin

A sand trap and a water feature at the Wynn Golf Club

5 Las Vegas Paiute Golf Resort

Snow Mountain, Highway 95 (exit 95), 20 miles (32 km) N. of Las Vegas ▪ 800 711 2833

Set in the desert landscape, this was the first master-planned multicourse golf resort laid out on Native American land. There are three courses in total: Snow Mountain, Sun Mountain, and The Wolf, all devised by Pete Dye, who has designed many esteemed courses.

6 Desert Willow Golf Course

2020 W. Horizon Ridge Parkway, Henderson ▪ 702 263 4653

This challenging 18-hole, 60-par course is 3,811 yards (3,485 m) long. Carved from the foothills of the Black Mountains, it is also surrounded by hazards and hilly terrain.

Entrance sign of Bali Hai Golf Club

7 Las Vegas National Golf Club

MAP D4 ▪ 1911 E. Desert Inn Rd ▪ 702 889 1000

Tiger Woods played at this golf course, established in 1961, on the path to his first PGA (Professional Golf Association) victory in 1996. Soft spikes are required on this course.

8 Wynn Golf Club

MAP N2–3 ▪ Wynn Las Vegas, 3131 Las Vegas Blvd ▪ 702 770 4653

The Wynn is the only Las Vegas casino to boast its own golf course, located just off the Strip. It underwent extensive redesign with elevation changes and water hazards.

9 Bali Hai Golf Club

MAP C5 ▪ 5160 Las Vegas Blvd S. ▪ 702 597 2400, 866 330 5178

This course is in a prime position, just steps away from Four Seasons Hotel Las Vegas and Mandalay Bay. The South Seas–inspired design (by Brian Curley and Lee Schmidt, two well-recognized golf course architects) features 2,500 thick stands of palm trees, 7 acres (2.8 ha) of large water hazards, and about 100,000 tropical plants and flowers.

10 Revere Golf Club

2600 Hampton Rd, Henderson ▪ 702 259 4653, 877 273 8373

Winding through three desert canyons, this course features natural changes in elevation and spectacular views of the Las Vegas skyline. The summer rates, as at many Las Vegas courses, are lower than during other seasons.

🔟 Spas and Health Clubs

Rome, the spa incorporates Roman baths and other touches of imperial luxury. In addition to the myriad treatments on offer for both men and women, there is a fitness center, and several wet rooms.

4 Sahra Spa at The Cosmopolitan

MAP Q2 ■ 3708 Las Vegas Blvd S. ■ 702 698 7000

The indulgent massages at Sahra include the Aromatherapy Massage, which uses desert-inspired essential oils; the Therapeutic Stone Massage done with perfectly warmed smooth stones; Mana Lomi, based on the Hawaiian healing concepts of working with the body, mind, and spirit; and the Signature Massage, combining Thai, Swedish, and Shiatsu techniques. There are also facials, body scrubs, and fitness classes.

5 The Spa at The Mirage

MAP P1–2 ■ The Mirage, 3400 Las Vegas Blvd S. ■ 702 791 7146

Feel your stresses and strains ebb away at this beautifully designed spa with its calming, neutral decor. There is an indulgent menu of treatments, and a salon just next door, including a barbershop for men.

1 Canyon Ranch Spa + Fitness

MAP P2 ■ The Venetian, 3355 Las Vegas Blvd S. ■ 702 414 3600

Residents at The Venetian can enjoy the 100-plus spa services, including skin-care treatments and 20 different styles of massage. The huge facility is also open to non-residents, as is the Canyon Ranch Grill. There is a full-service salon and an expansive co-ed lounging area.

2 Spa Aquae

MAP A3 ■ J. W. Marriott Las Vegas, 221 N. Rampart Blvd ■ 702 869 7807

Treatments at this spa are not solely focused on achieving external beauty. Rather, the tailor-made spa experiences are meant to enhance health and wellness. They make use of environmentally friendly products and each experience lasts long after guests leave. Make sure you try the ayurvedic treatments.

3 Qua Baths and Spa at Caesars Palace

MAP P1–2 ■ Caesars Palace, 3570 Las Vegas Blvd S. ■ 866 782 0655

With a style that recaptures the glorious splendor that was ancient

Calming decor of the spa at The Mirage

The sophisticated and luxurious spa suite at the ARIA Resort & Casino

6 The Spa at ARIA
MAP Q1–2 ■ ARIA Resort, 3730 Las Vegas Blvd S. ■ 702 590 9600

The luxurious spa at ARIA features Japanese heated-stone ganbanyoku beds, which help to purge toxins and stimulate circulation. In the Shio Salt Room guests can breathe in therapeutic salt air. In addition, there is a co-ed outdoor therapy pool on the balcony that overlooks the resort's remaining three pools and a fitness center, which offers personal training.

7 MGM Grand Spa
MAP R2 ■ MGM Grand, 3799 Las Vegas Blvd S. ■ 702 891 3077

Pamper yourself with a "Dreaming Ritual" package, which offers a foot soak, a massage, and a mud therapy treatment set to Aboriginal music. Alternatively, the excellent body exfoliation services take place in a wet room and include use of a Vichy shower, while the Morning Latte scrub is one of the signature services. You can purchase day passes for the workout room, sauna, and Jacuzzi. There's also a top hair salon overlooking the pool.

8 Spa & Salon at Bellagio
MAP Q1–2 ■ Bellagio, 3600 Las Vegas Blvd S. ■ 702 693 7472

This Italianate pampering palace combines elegant marble with cutting-edge fitness equipment. The spa's signature treatment is the Bellagio Stone Massage, which combines specially "harvested" stones prepared in a hydrobath with an energy-balancing technique to provide a thoroughly relaxing experience. Service is attentive.

9 The Spa & Salon at New York-New York
MAP R1–2 ■ New York-New York, 3790 Las Vegas Blvd S. ■ 702 740 6955

It will take far longer than a New York minute to enjoy all that is on offer at this spa. Relaxing treatments include the Chocolate-Covered Strawberry Bliss Scrub, Gel Lacquer Manicure, and the Escape Aging Facial. There's also a hair and beauty salon.

The lavish spa at Encore

10 The Spa at Encore
MAP N2 ■ Encore Las Vegas, 3121 Las Vegas Blvd S. ■ 702 770 3900

For a truly lavish spa experience, few places compare to the designer treatment rooms, garden villas, and couples' rooms here. The attention to detail is impeccable.

Following pages The Venetian's canal

🔟 Children's Attractions

① Adventuredome

This indoor amusement park *(see p52)* in the Circus Circus resort has an extensive array of rides and games designed to keep kids as well as adults entertained for hours. They can ride the Canyon Blaster, a looping roller coaster, or the Drifters, a Ferris wheel that simulates a hot-air balloon. Riders should expect plenty of twists and drops on the El Loco roller coaster.

El Loco roller coaster, Adventuredome

② Pepsi Ice Arena

MAP B2 ■ 2400 N. Rancho Dr ■ Open daily, hours vary ■ www.sobeicearenafr.com ■ Adm

This NHL-regulation-sized rink offers both figure skating and ice hockey facilities, as well as skate rental and lessons.

③ Siegfried & Roy's Secret Garden and Dolphin Habitat

MAP P1–2 ■ The Mirage, 3400 Las Vegas Blvd S. ■ 702 791 7188 ■ Open 10am–6pm daily ■ Adm

These two attractions come as a package, combining education and entertainment. Watch the dolphins swimming from above then use the tunnel for underwater viewing. The Secret Garden is an oasis of trees and greenery, with residents including white tigers, leopards, and rare white lions.

④ Fun Dungeon

MAP R1–2 ■ Excalibur, 3850 Las Vegas Blvd S. ■ Open 4–10pm Mon–Tue (to 11pm Wed–Thu), noon–11pm Fri–Sun

Located on the lower level of the Excalibur hotel and casino, this collection of over 200 rides and games includes several old classics, as well as new, high-tech video games. The arcade offers 15 carnival midways, 106 prize redemption games, 10 sports games, and 60 arcade games, such as the Mega Stacker, Big Bass, and Key Master.

⑤ Shark Reef Aquarium

MAP R1–2 ■ Mandalay Bay, 3950 Las Vegas Blvd S. ■ 702 632 7777 ■ Open 10am–6pm daily ■ Adm

This is North America's only predator-based aquarium with over 2,000 creatures in 1.6 million gallons (6 million litres) of water. Fifteen species of sharks, as well as crocodiles, giant rays, piranha, jellyfish, and sawfish surround visitors as they walk through an underwater acrylic tunnel.

Display in Avengers S.T.A.T.I.O.N.

6 Avengers S.T.A.T.I.O.N.

MAP P2 ■ Treasure Island, 3300 Las Vegas Blvd S. ■ 702 894 7626 ■ 11am–6pm daily ■ Adm

This family-friendly attraction, suitable for all ages, delves into the history and profiles of Captain America, Hulk, Thor, and Iron Man. On display are Captain America's uniform and shield, Bruce Banner's laboratory, Vision's birth cradle, the uniforms and weapons of Hawkeye and Black Widow, and Iron Man's MK 45 suit and The Hulkbuster suit.

7 Flamingo Wildlife Habitat

MAP P2 ■ Flamingo Las Vegas, 3555 Las Vegas Blvd S. ■ 702 733 3349 ■ Open dawn–dusk daily

Step through the doors and you'll be transported to a place of lush foliage, water birds, and other animals. The creatures all live on islands and in streams surrounded by stunning landscape and water-falls, and are cared for by a team of experts. Walk among flamingoes, swans, ducks, turtles, pelicans, and koi in this quiet escape from the hectic Strip. Native hummingbirds, year-round residents, provide close encounters at several feeders.

8 Las Vegas Mini Gran Prix

MAP A2 ■ 1401 N. Rainbow Blvd ■ 702 500 1794 ■ Open 11am–9pm Mon–Thu (to 10pm Fri), 10am–10pm Sat (to 9pm Sun) ■ Adm

Adult Gran Prix cars, sprint karts, go-karts, kiddie karts, plus the Dragon Coaster, Super Slide, and lots of arcade games make this a favorite off-Strip destination for Las Vegas kids as well as visitors.

9 DISCOVERY Children's Museum

MAP K3 ■ Donald W. Reynolds Discovery Center, 360 Promenade Place ■ 702 382 5437 ■ Open 10am–5pm Tue–Sat ■ Adm

West of Downtown, this museum features 58,000 sq ft (5,388 sq m) of educational space. Its centerpiece, the 60-ft (18-m) Summit Tower, is filled with experimentative science exhibits and a new DISCOVERY Lab to stimulate hands-on creativity.

10 Red Rock Lanes

MAP A3 ■ Red Rock Resort, 11011 W. Charleston Ave ■ 702 797 7777 ■ Open 9am–midnight (to 2am Fri–Sat) daily ■ Adm

This 72-lane bowling center comes equipped with a great sound system, lighting effects, fog machines, image generators, and disco balls to turn an ordinary afternoon into a party.

A bowler at Red Rock Lanes

🔟 Thrill Rides and Simulators

The Canyon Blaster roller coaster at Adventuredome

1 Adventuredome
MAP M–N2 ■ Circus Circus, 2880 Las Vegas Blvd S. ■ 702 794 3939 ■ Open daily, hours vary ■ Adm

There are several fun rides to sample at Adventuredome, Circus Circus's indoor theme park. Possibly the most exciting ride is the high-speed Canyon Blaster, which is billed as "the only double-loop, double-corkscrew indoor roller coaster." Disk'O is a rocking and spinning ride accompanied by loud disco music.

2 Big Shot
MAP L–M3 ■ Stratosphere Tower, 2000 Las Vegas Blvd S.

Located on the USA's tallest observation tower, the Big Shot shoots riders 160 ft (50 m) into the air. They then free-fall back to the launchpad. It's not a ride for the faint hearted, or for kids. Ride at night for a great view of the Strip.

3 The Desperado
MAP T2 ■ Buffalo Bill's, 31900 Las Vegas Blvd S., Primm Valley, 35 miles (56 km) south of Las Vegas on I-5 ■ 702 386 7867 ■ Height restrictions

Billed as one of the fastest roller coasters in the US, the Desperado reaches speeds of up to 90 mph (145 kph). Try to catch the great views of the Primm Valley from the highest point. If that is too daring for you, try the arcade with action-packed video and pinball games, or get drenched on the Adventure Canyon Log Flume.

4 SlotZilla Zip Line
MAP K4 ■ Fremont St

This colossal slot machine launches two tiers of riders – some lying prone in harnesses, others seated – to fly beneath the canopy of Downtown's Fremont Street Experience.

(5) Airline Captain for a Day
MAP E5 ▪ 1771 Whitney Mesa Dr. Henderson ▪ 702 529 4806

Take control of a full motion flight simulator and feel what it's like to pilot a real Boeing 737. This 30-minute experience takes place in the same simulators where pilots train.

(6) SkyJump Las Vegas
MAP L–M3 ▪ Stratosphere Tower, 2000 Las Vegas Blvd S. ▪ 702 380 7777 ▪ Age restrictions

This "controlled free fall" lets brave souls jump 855 ft (261 m) from the 108th floor of the Stratosphere on to a landing mat. Jumpers reach 40 mph (64 kph) as they soar through the air before landing with their feet back on the ground. Purchase a package deal to jump both at night and during the day.

(7) The Big Apple Coaster
MAP R1–2 ▪ New York–New York, 3790 Las Vegas Blvd S.

For those more thrill-seeking riders who dare to keep their eyes open during this white-knuckler, the Coney Island-style ride offers spectacular views of the Strip. The coaster route writhes, dips, dives, and loops around the resort's perimeter. While riding, you'll drop 144 ft (44 m) and hit speeds of 67 mph (108 kph).

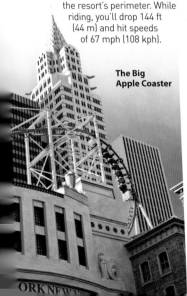

The Big Apple Coaster

High Roller above The LINQ fountains

(8) High Roller
MAP P2 ▪ The LINQ, 3535 Las Vegas Blvd S.

The second tallest observation wheel in the world, the High Roller stands at a height of 550 ft (168 m) and is located at the heart of the Strip. It provides fantastic views of the city from the top.

(9) Vegas Indoor Skydiving
MAP N3 ▪ 200 Convention Center Dr ▪ 702 731 4768

Vegas Indoor Skydiving advises potential customers that skydiving is not without risk, but this is a great place to gain wings without the use of an airplane or a parachute. The one-hour experience includes training and a simulated skydive in a vertical wind tunnel complete with a mesh trampoline wall and foam-padded walls.

(10) Richard Petty Driving Experience
MAP E1 ▪ Las Vegas Motor Speedway, 7000 Las Vegas Blvd N. ▪ 704 886 2400

After instruction, participants can get into the driver's seat of an authentic NASCAR-style stock car, and go, go, go! Even if you can't drive, a passenger-seat ride is also available.

🔟 Casinos

1 Plaza Hotel and Casino

Housed in the former railway station of Las Vegas, facing directly along Fremont Street, the enormous Plaza Hotel and Casino *(see p93)* has reinvented itself in recent years to provide once again the quintessential Downtown gambling experience, which is much less slick than what you will find on the Strip. Sports betting has been on offer here for longer than at any other casino in the city, and now also includes a Race and Sports Book run by William Hill.

2 Park MGM

MAP Q1–2 ▪ **3770 Las Vegas Blvd S.** ▪ **702 730 7777** ▪ **www. parkmgm.mgmresorts.com**

A chic reboot of the venerable Monte Carlo, this glitzy casino adjoining the state-of-the-art 5,200-seat Park Theater, boasts over 60 game tables and 1,300 new slot machines. Park MGM offers an exclusive Sports Book with a bar & grill and a pool table.

3 El Cortez

MAP K4 ▪ **600 E. Fremont St** ▪ **702 385 5200** ▪ **www.elcortezhotel casino.com**

The definitive Downtown casino, a short walk east of the roofed

and pedestrianized blocks of Fremont Street, is renowned for the low odds on its gaming tables and its (relatively) high-paying slot machines. If you like your gambling hard-bitten, this is the place to come. Although renovated to 21st-century standards, it's on the National Register of Historic Places.

The lit-up exterior of El Cortez

4 Circa Resort & Casino

Opened in 2020 on the former site of the Las Vegas Club, this two-story casino and hotel *(p95)* holds 1,350 slot machines and 49 table games including blackjack, roulette, craps, baccarat, and three-card poker. There are also private seats at stadium-style electronic table games. Most noteworthy is its massive Sports Book, reputed to be the largest in the world, with a 1,000-person viewing capacity and a state-of-the-art three-story high-definition screen.

5 Sunset Station

Primarily patronized by local residents, Sunset Station is located just across from the Galleria at Sunset shopping mall. The casino benefits from plenty of natural light and is well ventilated, too. It also has a Kids' Quest (nursery), where regular play events, with themes such as Superheroes and Comic Capers, are run *(see p100)*.

⑥ Virgin Hotels Las Vegas
MAP Q3 ■ 4455 Paradise Rd
■ 702 693 5000 ■ www.mohegan
sunlasvegas.com

Situated about a mile to the east of the Strip, this hotel is owned by British billionaire Richard Branson, but its casino is operated by the Mohegan Sun casino chain. The casino has on offer more than 650 slot machines and over 50 table games, including blackjack, roulette, baccarat, craps, pai gow, and three-card-poker.

⑦ Bellagio
Ranking among the plushest of all the major Strip casinos, Bellagio (see pp14–15) offers as swanky a gaming experience as you could ever hope to find. There are exclusive baccarat and poker areas reserved for high rollers, and video games inlaid into the marble counters. It is a great place to take advantage of the Las Vegas custom whereby active gamblers are plied with free drinks.

⑧ Golden Nugget
MAP K4 ■ 129 E. Fremont St
■ 702 385 7111 ■ www.golden
nugget.com

This casino sets itself apart from its Downtown neighbors as it displays the world's largest (Hand of Faith) gold nugget. The restaurants are very good, and the casino is a pleasant place to gamble while waiting to see the Fremont Street Experience (see p91), which takes place just outside the doors of the complex.

Harrah's casino sign

⑨ Harrah's
MAP P2 ■ 3475 Las Vegas Blvd S. ■ 702 369 5000 ■ www.caesars.com/harrahs

One of the most respected names in the gaming industry, Caesars has more than a dozen properties across the US, and this one in particular offers value for money in service, food, and ambience. Harrah's has one of the best player's clubs as far as prizes are concerned. The club card can be used at any Caesars property.

⑩ The Cosmopolitan
MAP Q2 ■ 3708 Las Vegas Blvd S. ■ 702 698 7000 ■ www.cosmopolitanlasvegas.com

There is no more electrifying and energizing casino in Las Vegas than the vibrant, buzzing Cosmopolitan – especially late on a weekend evening, when its clubs and bars are packed to the point of bursting. The Cosmopolitan, with its excellent service, does its utmost to prevent anyone from leaving, and the big-game atmosphere in its Race and Sports Book is unbeatable.

The vibrant interior of the Cosmopolitan casino

🔟 Gambling in Las Vegas

"Progressive" slot machines, with their shared jackpot rising

① Slot Machines
While today's slot machines are sophisticated computers, rather than one-armed bandits, the principle is the same as ever. The casinos offer a payback of 85–95 per cent, but the hope of a jackpot keeps gamblers playing. On "progressive" machines, which are linked across Nevada by microchip, the progressive jackpot grows rapidly, as every player in the state contributes to it.

② Blackjack
In blackjack – also known as pontoon – each player is dealt two cards, then tries to create a hand adding nearly, or exactly, to 21. The aim is also to beat the dealer, who builds his own hand following fixed rules. There is a "correct" strategy for every situation, but the system is hard to learn.

③ Poker
Most poker players in Las Vegas play either Seven-Card Stud or Texas Hold 'Em, and thus compete against whoever is seated at the same table – so beware, you may be playing with experts. If you would

Caesars Palace poker chip

rather play against the casino, choose a format like Let It Ride or Pai Gow Poker.

④ Wheel of Fortune
This sideshow game is designed to lure in non-gamblers. The dealer spins a large wheel that is divided into segments marked with different amounts. When the wheel stops, an arrow indicates the winning segment. For each dollar you bet on that amount, you win that many dollars. The odds, though, are poor.

⑤ Roulette
The classic game of pure chance, roulette lets players bet on which slot in a numbered, spinning wheel a dropped ball will land on. For the best odds, look for a wheel that holds just one "0," and not, like most in Las Vegas, a "00" slot as well.

⑥ Bingo
The game consists of getting five numbers in a row called (and all spots on the blackout finale game), which can be marked off with ink daubers or electronic tablets. Offered primarily

in downtown and local casinos, an hour's session can be bought for $4–5, during which players get complimentary drinks and snacks.

7 Baccarat

Baccarat is a quick-fire card game requiring no skill and offering (relatively) good odds. Most casinos only offer it to big-stakes gamblers – and it's from baccarat-loving high-rollers that they rake in almost half of their table-gaming revenue.

8 Sports Betting

Free drinks are offered to punters at Sports Books after they've made a minimum bet. Small wonder that the "Race and Sports Book" in each casino is usually packed, with a party atmosphere for major events.

9 Keno

Keno is a bingo-like game; each player chooses up to twenty numbers between 1 and 80. Match five or more of the twenty drawn by the casino, and you win small; match all twenty and you win big.

Craps players at Golden Nugget

10 Craps

More than any other casino game, craps feels like a team game; players cluster excitedly around the high-walled table to whoop and roar as one throws the dice and the rest lay their bets. Take a free lesson if you don't know the rules – you could never learn by watching.

TOP 10 CASINOS FOR FREE GAMBLING LESSONS

Circus Circus sign

1 Circus Circus
Daily lessons: blackjack, craps, roulette and poker (see p87).

2 Plaza Hotel Casino
Craps lessons Mon–Thu at 4pm (p93).

3 Excalibur
Daily lessons: poker at 11am; roulette at 11am and 7pm; blackjack at 11:30am and 7:30pm; and craps at 11:30am and 8pm (see p41).

4 Golden Nugget
Daily lessons: poker at 10am; craps at 10am; Pai Gow Poker at 10:30am; roulette at 11:30am; and blackjack at noon (see p55).

5 Luxor
Daily lessons: poker at 10am; roulette, craps, and blackjack at noon (see p40).

6 New York New York
Daily lessons: craps at 11am; blackjack at noon (see p41).

7 Mandalay Bay
MAP R1 ▪ 3950 Las Vegas Blvd S.
Daily poker lessons at 2pm.

8 Stratosphere
Daily lessons: poker at 8pm Sat & Sun (see p87).

9 South Point
MAP C5 ▪ 9777 Las Vegas Blvd S.
▪ www.southpointcasino.com
Craps lessons: held at 10:15am Tue and Thu and 11:15am Sat.

10 The Venetian
Some of the best free lessons on gambling in Las Vegas take place at this spacious casino; Mon–Fri: craps at 11am; blackjack at 11:30am (see pp16–17).

📟 Shows

1 O
MAP Q1–2 ■ Bellagio, 3600 Las Vegas Blvd S. ■ 888 488 7111 for tickets

O, staged by Cirque du Soleil, is a circus quite unlike any other. The whole show revolves around the theme of water (hence the name, as in the French *eau*). The acrobats, synchronized swimmers, divers, and characters perform in, on, and above water. Seven hydraulic lifts raise and lower the water levels throughout the performance, allowing for spectacular diving and other feats.

Trapeze act during a performance of *O*

2 Mystère
MAP P2 ■ Treasure Island, 3300 Las Vegas Blvd S. ■ 800 392 1999, 702 894 7722 for tickets

Created for Treasure Island, *Mystère* is an enchanting circus that – like all Cirque du Soleil productions – has a mystical thread running through it. The costumes are innovative and colorful, and together with the high-energy acrobatics, evocative dances, and vivid lighting, create an overwhelming sensory experience.

3 Penn & Teller
MAP P1 ■ Rio All-Suite Hotel and Casino, 3700 W. Flamingo Rd ■ 702 777 2782

Known as "The Bad Boys of Magic" for revealing the secrets of their tricks, Penn & Teller manage to break all of the rules of magic in this show. Edgy, provocative, and hilarious, on any given night the act can involve knives, guns, a fire-eating showgirl, or a duck. The show relies on audience participation, with members invited onto the stage to take part in tricks.

4 Absinthe
MAP P1–2 ■ Caesars Palace, 3570 Las Vegas Blvd S. ■ 855 234 7469

This adults-only show is a blend of carnival and spectacle, featuring wild and outlandish acts accompanied by outrageous humor in a theater-in-the-round presentation under a big top outside Caesars. Audiences are awed by the acts performed.

5 Hypnosis Unleashed
MAP K4 ■ 202 Fremont St ■ 702 385 4011 ■ www.fourqueens.com

Dubbed the "Rock Star of Hypnosis" due to his high energy, Kevin Lepine infuses fast-paced hypnosis with stand-up comedy, razor-sharp wit, and genuine empathy. Recommended for ages 18 and above.

6 KÀ
MAP R2 ■ MGM Grand, 3799 Las Vegas Blvd S. ■ 702 531 3826, 866 740 7711

This innovative theatrical spectacle from Cirque du Soleil features astonishing acrobatic performances, martial arts, puppetry, multimedia, and pyrotechnics. The colorful and entertaining show was inspired by the Egyptian belief in the *kà*, an invisible spiritual body that accompanies a person throughout their life. This theme is developed into an exciting tale of imperial twins who undertake a perilous journey into mystical lands. They must face several challenges

Wax statues of the Blue Man Group at Madame Tussauds

before they can fulfill their destiny. Impressive computer-generated effects and 80 outstanding performers bring the stage to life.

7 Tournament of Kings
MAP R1–2 ■ Excalibur, 3850 Las Vegas Blvd S. ■ 702 597 7600

The long-running Tournament of Kings is filled with live jousting, song and dance, combat, entertainment, and crowd participation. While King Arthur and his team of knights put on a show inside an arena, you can enjoy a dinner of Cornish hen with potatoes, corn on the cob, fresh biscuits, and apple square dessert.

8 Blue Man Group
MAP R1 ■ Luxor, 3900 Las Vegas Blvd S. ■ 702 262 4400

Unique, funny, wildly innovative, and with a contagious energy, this show is part parade and part dance party. Heralded by three bald and blue men, the show features comedy, drums, paint, and technology. It is popular with children and adults alike.

9 Terry Fator
MAP R1–2 ■ New York-New York, 3790 Las Vegas Blvd S. ■ 866 606 7111

America's Got Talent winner Terry Fator combines comedy with music, ventriloquism, and hilarious celebrity impressions to create a unique brand of entertainment. His puppet co-stars include Emma Taylor, "the little girl with the big voice"; Maynard Thompkins, the Elvis Impersonator; and Duggie Scott Walker, the annoying neighbor.

10 The Beatles LOVE
MAP P1–2 ■ The Mirage, 3400 Las Vegas Blvd S. ■ 702 792 7777, 800 963 9634

First staged in 2006, this theatrical production has Cirque du Soleil combining its magic with the exuberant spirit and timeless music of one of the best-loved bands in the world.

🔟 Music and Performing Arts Venues

Panoramic view of Allegiant Stadium

1 Allegiant Stadium

MAP R1 ▪ 3333 Al Davis Way ▪ 725 780 2000 ▪ www.allegiant stadium.com

While this massive 65,000-seat stadium is often used for the Las Vegas Raiders and University of Nevada, Las Vegas home football games, major concerts are also held here. Pop and rock performers have included Garth Brooks and Guns N' Roses. The stadium is within walking distance of Mandalay Bay, New York-New York, and Park MGM.

2 Michelob ULTRA Arena

MAP R2 ▪ 3950 Las Vegas Blvd S. ▪ 702 632 7777 ▪ www.mandalay bay.mgmresorts.com

Planet Hollywood sign

Luciano Pavarotti inaugurated the 12,000-seat events center in 1999. Since then, performers as diverse as tenor Andrea Bocelli (with the Russian Symphony Orchestra), Justin Timberlake, and Kanye West have graced its stage. During one month in particular, the Michelob ULTRA Arena was exceptionally eclectic, staging as it did a heavyweight bout between Evander Holyfield and John Ruiz, figure skater Katarina Witt's *Kisses on Ice* show, and a vocal performance by Andrea Bocelli.

3 The Smith Center for the Performing Arts

MAP K3 ▪ 361 Symphony Park Ave ▪ 702 749 2000 ▪ www. thesmithcenter.com

Featuring a 2,050-seat hall with brilliant acoustics, cabaret jazz stage, and intimate theater space, The Smith Center showcases full seasons of dance, music, and spoken word performances, and Broadway shows. Take the time to visit Symphony Park in front of the hall and browse the artworks inside as well.

4 The Theater at Virgin Hotels Las Vegas

MAP Q3 ▪ Virgin Hotels Las Vegas, 4455 Paradise Rd ▪ 702 693 5222

When the Hard Rock Hotel transitioned into Virgin Hotels in 2018, so did its concert venue, previously called The Joint. The 4,500-seat theater still hosts rock and roll acts but has also added other genres to its line-up, including performances by Journey, Daughtry, and Lizzo.

5 AXIS Theater at Planet Hollywood

The 6,700-seat theater at Planet Hollywood Resort & Casino *(see p41)* features performances by Pitbull, Jennifer Lopez, and the Backstreet Boys.

6 T-Mobile Arena

MAP Q1 ▪ The Park Las Vegas, 3780 Las Vegas Blvd S. ▪ 702 692 1600 ▪ www.t-mobilearena.com

Opened in 2016, the T-Mobile Arena boasts 20,000 seats, and hosts events such as UFC, boxing, basketball, and hockey – it is the home ground for

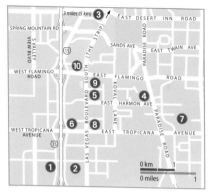

the Vegas Golden Knights NHL hockey team. High-profile award shows and concerts by artists such as Jay-Z, Imagine Dragons, and Lady Gaga are also held here.

7 Thomas & Mack Center

MAP Q4 ■ University of Nevada Las Vegas, S. Maryland Parkway ■ 702 739 3267 ■ www.thomasand mack.com

Initially designed for college basketball, over the years the Thomas & Mack Center has become a site for major boxing matches as well as professional football and basketball tournaments. It has previously hosted the Vegoose Music Festival, and is one of the largest arenas in the city. In addition, the National Finals Rodeo is held here annually, drawing tens of thousands of fans. Family-style entertainment and concerts are just as popular as the sporting events.

8 David Copperfield Theater and Grand Garden Arena

MAP R2 ■ MGM Grand Hotel, 3799 Las Vegas Blvd S. ■ 866 740 7711 ■ www.mgmgrand.com/ entertainment

Headliners such as Tom Jones and music acts like Sting and Aerosmith regularly appear at the 740-seat David Copperfield Theater. MGM's larger 16,800-seat special-events center, the Grand Garden Arena,

is used for superstar concerts, major sporting events, and other spectaculars. It was the setting for Barbra Streisand's Millennium Concert on New Year's Eve 1999, and has since hosted numerous high-profile concerts.

9 Paris Theater

MAP Q2 ■ Paris Las Vegas, 3655 Las Vegas Blvd S. ■ 877 796 2096

This Parisian-style theater opened in 1999 and has welcomed big names ever since, including Dennis Miller, Bobby Vinton, and Earth, Wind & Fire. It has also hosted the Broadway production of *The Producers* and *America's Got Talent* finale.

The auditorium of The Colosseum

10 The Colosseum

MAP P1–2 ■ Caesars Palace, 3570 Las Vegas Blvd S. ■ 702 866 1400 ■ www.thecolosseum.com

Originally built to accommodate a multi-year engagement by the stellar Celine Dion, Caesars' astonishing Colosseum with 4,000 seats, right beside the Strip, remains one of the top entertainment venues in the world. Stars such as Sting, Rod Stewart, and Mariah Carey stage spectacular long-term residencies here, while touring acts, as well as big-name comedians like Jerry Seinfeld, regularly drop in for one-off shows.

TOP 10 Nightclubs

Revellers during NightSwim at Encore Beach Club

1 Jewel
MAP Q1 ▪ ARIA, 3730
Las Vegas Blvd S. ▪ 702 590 8000
▪ Open 10:30pm–4am Fri–Sat ▪ Adm
▪ jewelnightclub.com

This spacious club is lined with
LED ribbons just above the dance
floor and has a mesmerizing wall
of light that shape-shifts and shines
just behind the DJ booth. The design
offers clear views and vantage points
in every direction, meaning that you
can see and be seen. Five themed
VIP suites circle the mezzanine, providing an immersive experience.

2 Encore Beach Club
MAP N2 ▪ Wynn Las Vegas,
3131 Las Vegas Blvd S. ▪ 702 770
7300 ▪ Open Mar–Oct: 11am–6pm
Thu–Sun ▪ Adm ▪ www.encore
beachclub.com

A "dayclub" rather than a nightclub
that is open, for obvious reasons,
in summer only – the ultra-lavish
Encore Beach Club is basically a
no-expense-spared all-day pool
party, given the royal seal of approval
by Prince Harry in 2012.

3 TAO Nightclub
MAP P2 ▪ The Venetian,
3377 Las Vegas Blvd S. ▪ 702 388
8588 ▪ Open 10:30pm–5am Thu–
Sat; Beach Club: 11:30am–6pm
daily in summer ▪ Adm ▪ www.
taolasvegas.com

Originally a celeb-filled Asian
bistro in New York, TAO received
a Vegas makeover at The Venetian
(see pp16–17) to become the fifth
highest-earning nightclub in the
US. Besides its restaurant and bars,
the major features of this Chinese,
Japanese, and Thai-themed club are
waterfalls, giant Buddha statues, and
an artificial sandy beach. In summer,
the pool turns into the TAO Beach
club. The dance floor is small, but
big-name guest DJs keep the place
packed every weekend.

4 On the Record

MAP Q2 ■ Park MGM 3770 Las Vegas Blvd S. ■ 702 730 6773 ■ Open 10:30pm–3am Wed, Fri & Sat ■ www.ontherecordlv.com

Not your ordinary Vegas nightclub, On the Record gets its name from being hidden behind a record store, but its actual entrance is off Park MGM's main casino floor. It features both indoor and outdoor spaces, a double-decker bus which hosts DJ sets, and karaoke rooms for renting.

5 Chateau Nightclub

MAP Q2 ■ Paris Las Vegas, 3655 Las Vegas Blvd S. ■ 702 776 7777 ■ Open 10pm–2am Thu–Sat ■ Adm ■ www.chateaunights.com

Spanning more than 45,000 sq ft (4,181 sq m) and sprawled across two stories, the Chateau offers two unique nightlife experiences, including a high-energy outdoor nightclub with views of the Eiffel Tower above and the Bellagio Fountains across the street.

6 XS

MAP N2 ■ Encore Las Vegas, 3131 Las Vegas Blvd S. ■ 702 770 7300 ■ Open 10:30pm–4am Fri–Sun ■ Adm ■ www.xslasvegas.com

Named the number one nightclub in the US by Nightclub and Bar's Top 100 for several years, this nightspot features top-of-the-line production elements, including pyrotechnics, LEDs, lasers, and an in-the-round DJ booth that can be seen from anywhere in the club.

7 MARQUEE

MAP Q1 ■ The Cosmopolitan, 3708 Las Vegas Blvd S. ■ 702 333 9000 ■ Open 10pm–5am Fri & Sat, 11am–sunset daily in summer ■ Adm ■ www.marqueelasvegas.com

This massive 60,000-sq-ft nightclub holds seven bars and three distinct rooms – the Main Room, the Boombox, and the Library – as well as an open-air, poolside "dayclub" in summer. The dress code is upscale casual; buttoned shirts with collars and dress shoes for gentlemen.

8 Omnia

MAP P1–2 ■ Caesars Palace, 3570 Las Vegas Blvd S. ■ 702 785 6200 ■ Open 10:30pm–4am Tue & Fri–Sun ■ Adm ■ www.omnianightclub.com

Jaws dropped when Caesars Palace unveiled this high-tech, state-of-the-art nightclub in 2015, to replace the much-lamented Pure. As well as a constantly changing roster of big-name EDM DJs, it incorporates a vast Strip-view roof terrace.

9 Hakkasan

MAP R2 ■ MGM Grand, 3799 Las Vegas Blvd S. ■ 702 891 3838 ■ Open 10:30pm–4am Thu–Sat ■ Adm ■ www.hakkasannightclub.com

Of course Las Vegas is home to nightclubs, though arguably this sprawling complex is really two clubs, plus several lounges and bars. On a big night, 3,300 revelers squeeze in.

10 Drai's

MAP P2 ■ The Cromwell, 3595 Las Vegas Blvd S. ■ 702 777 3800 ■ Open 10pm–3am Fri–Sun; Drai's Beach Club: open 10am–6pm Thu–Sun in summer ■ Adm ■ www.draislv.com

This colossal club, open both day and night during the summer, enjoys fabulous views of the Strip from its prime position on the Cromwell's specially strengthened roof, and features live performers as well as DJs.

Outdoor rooftop pools at Drai's

🔟 Bars and Lounges on the Strip

Overlook Lounge

1 Overlook Lounge

MAP N2 ■ Wynn Las Vegas, 3131 Las Vegas Blvd S. ■ Open 2pm–1am Mon–Thu, noon–1am Fri–Sun

This matching pair of colorful, classy cocktail bars, set one above the other on the central stairwell of Wynn Las Vegas (see pp18–19), are playfully decorated with bright umbrellas. They give a great vantage point for the nightly light and music show on the Lake of Dreams.

2 Skyfall Lounge

MAP R2 ■ Delano Las Vegas 3940 S. Las Vegas Blvd ■ 877 632 5400 ■ Open 5pm–midnight Fri–Sun

This lounge on the top floor of the Delano Las Vegas is worth a visit for the view alone. The panoramic vistas of the city are among the best you'll find anywhere.

3 Peppermill Fireside Lounge

MAP N3 ■ 2985 Las Vegas Blvd S. ■ 702 735 4177 ■ Open 7am–11pm Sun–Wed (to 2am Thu–Sat)

This much-loved veteran bar is one of the few survivors of the Las Vegas that existed before the corporations moved in. However, with its pink neon, banquette seating, and flame-spouting fire pit, it is just as over-the-top as the casino lounges.

4 Nine Fine Irishmen

MAP R2 ■ New York–New York, 3790 Las Vegas Blvd S. ■ 702 740 3311 ■ Open noon–1am Mon–Thu, 11am–2am Fri, 10am–2am Sat, 10am–1am Sun ■ Adm

This casino bar in New York–New York (see p40) is a great Irish pub. Everything here is shipped over from Ireland. There is nightly Irish entertainment, too.

5 Cleopatra's Barge

MAP P1–2 ■ Caesars Palace, 3570 Las Vegas Blvd S. ■ 702 731 7333 ■ Open 6–11pm Mon–Wed, 5pm–midnight Thu–Sat

This lounge bar, with ancient Egyptian decor, is located on a floating barge in the heart of Caesars Palace (see p40).

6 Chandelier

MAP Q2 ■ The Cosmopolitan, 3708 Las Vegas Blvd S. ■ 877 893 2003 ■ Open 24hr daily

A big, shimmering chandelier hangs down through three floors of the Cosmopolitan casino (see p55), and it is circled at all three levels by this chic bar. The uppermost level is a cool, relaxed lounge while the central level is a full-fledged nightclub.

The Cosmopolitan's Chandelier

(7) Gilley's Saloon

MAP P2 ▪ TI, 3300 Las Vegas Blvd S. ▪ 702 894 7111 ▪ Open 11–2am Sun–Thu (to 4am Fri & Sat) ▪ Adm for live music

There is always a party atmosphere in this lively bar where you can ride a mechanical rodeo bull, take a lesson in line dancing, or catch one of the live bands that frequently play here.

(8) Minus5° Ice Bar

MAP R1 ▪ Mandalay Bay, 3930 Las Vegas Blvd S. ▪ 702 740 5800 ▪ Open 11am–midnight Sun–Thu (to 1:30am Fri & Sat) ▪ Adm

Everything including the glasses, the seating, and even the bar is made of ice. Warm clothing is provided.

Decor made of ice at Minus5° Ice Bar

(9) Beerhaus

MAP Q1 ▪ The Park Las Vegas 3784 Las Vegas Blvd S. ▪ 702 692 2337 ▪ Open 11am–midnight Mon–Thu & Sun (to 1am Fri & Sat)

Located within The Park, this pub offers more than 60 craft beers with an emphasis on local brews. It's a popular hangout for before and after ice hockey games at the nearby T-Mobile Arena.

(10) The Dorsey

MAP P2 ▪ The Venetian, 3355 Las Vegas Blvd S. ▪ 702 414 1945 ▪ Open 4pm–2am daily

True cocktail culture is celebrated here, along with old school service standards. The handcrafted cocktail menu was designed by award-winning bartender Sam Ross. In the evenings, DJs spin both classics and new tunes.

TOP 10 LGBTQ+ VENUES

Melissa Molinaro at Piranha

1 Piranha
MAP C4 ▪ 4633 Paradise Rd
A lavish gay nightclub with state-of-the-art sound system and lighting.

2 FLEX
MAP B3 ▪ 4371 W Charleston Blvd
This cocktail lounge offers karaoke, dancing, and a game room.

3 Charleys
MAP B5 ▪ 5012 Arville St
Country-themed nightclub with karaoke, dancing, and drag queen bingo.

4 Spotlight Lounge
MAP M4 ▪ 975 E. Sahara Ave
This friendly spot has on offer daily drinks specials, pool tables, and shuffleboard tournaments on Saturdays.

5 Luxor
The LGBTQ+ progressive Luxor resort (see p40) hosts a weekly "Temptation Sunday" gay and lesbian pool party.

6 Free Zone
MAP C4 ▪ 60 E Naples Dr
Home to the city's longest-running drag show, every Friday and Saturday.

7 The Garage
MAP D4 ▪ 1487 E Flamingo Rde
At Garage, enjoy darts, DJs, karaoke, and plenty of TVs airing sports programing.

6 Phoenix Bar & Lounge
MAP M1 ▪ 4213 W. Sahara Ave
A laid back gay bar featuring drag shows, karaoke, and gaming.

9 Badlands Saloon
MAP C3 ▪ 953 E Sahara Ave
Enjoy drinks and theme nights that include a drag show on Friday.

10 Fun Hog Ranch
MAP C4 ▪ 495 E Twain
Leather and fetish-wear are "strongly encouraged" at this bar.

🔟 Gourmet Restaurants

① Le Cirque
MAP Q1–2 ■ Bellagio, 3600 Las Vegas Blvd S. ■ 702 693 8100 ■ Closed L daily ■ $$$

Renowned for its sumptuous French cuisine, this opulent and much-lauded restaurant, an offshoot of the Manhattan original, is set in a prime position by the Bellagio's lake (see pp14–15). The six-course tasting menu, available with wonderful wine pairings, abounds in caviar and truffles.

The classic Picasso restaurant

② Picasso
The room is exquisite, with original Picasso paintings and ceramics adorning the walls and a carpet designed by Pablo Picasso's son, Claude, underfoot. The Spanish-born chef, Julian Serrano, creates contemporary French dishes with an Iberian accent. Among the delights offered here (see p85) are Maine lobster salad, pan-seared scallop, sautéed steak of foie gras, and sautéed fillet of halibut. The wine cellar boasts 1,500 plus European labels as well.

③ Julian Serrano
MAP Q1 ■ ARIA Resort, 3730 Las Vegas Blvd S. ■ 877 230 2742 ■ $$$

This stylish, contemporary restaurant, adjoining the main lobby of the ARIA Resort (see p24), serves its namesake chef's take on Spanish tapas, with delectable interpretations of his native fare. Larger plates are available as well, including paella.

④ L'Atelier de Joël Robuchon
A feast for both the palate and the eyes, for a seat at the service counter will enable you to watch your food get prepared. The cuisine at this outstanding restaurant (see p85) is predominantly French, with Asian and Spanish influences. Signature dishes include L'Artichaut, a semi-soft boiled egg on a carbonara of pearl pasta with smoked bacon and baby artichoke.

⑤ Twist by Pierre Gagnaire
MAP Q2 ■ Waldorf Astoria, 3752 Las Vegas Blvd S. ■ 702 590 8888 ■ Closed daily L, Sun & Mon ■ $$$

Pierre Gagnaire, who is among the most inventive of the new generation of French chefs, "twists" classic dishes to create everything from sea-urchin mousse to foie gras ice cream. This is his only US outlet, set within the 5-star Waldorf Astoria hotel in CityCenter (see p25).

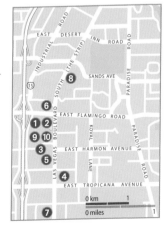

The sleek interior of Nobu

fetched by wine stewards (also called "wine angels"), who are raised and lowered on cables. The international menu includes steaks, seafood, pasta, and appetizers such as charred octopus and foie gras.

8 Bouchon
Established by one of the most brilliant chefs in America, Thomas Keller, this restaurant *(see p85)* serves up traditional French-bistro fare in a sunlit Gallic surroundings or outside in an airy patio. The food is cooked using only top-quality ingredients, and the unique wine list on offer ensures the perfect accompaniment to each dish.

6 Nobu
MAP P1 ■ Caesars Palace, 3570 Las Vegas Blvd S. ■ 702 785 6628 ■ Closed daily L ■ $$$
Diners all over the world simply cannot seem to resist the exquisite fusion cuisine of the Japanese-Peruvian chef Nobu Matsuhisa. Signature dishes include black cod miso, rock shrimp tempura and yellowtail *Sashimi*.

9 Estiatorio Milos
MAP P2 ■ The Venetian, 3355 Las Vegas Blvd S. ■ 702 414 1270 ■ $$$
This gorgeous Greek restaurant, decorated in true Classic style, specializes in delicately prepared fish, which are flown in specially each day from Athens. The lunch menu guarantees great value.

7 Aureole
MAP R1 ■ Mandalay Bay, 3950 Las Vegas Blvd S. ■ 702 632 7401 ■ Closed daily L ■ $$$
This restaurant by American celebrity chef Charlie Palmer is famous for its four-story wine tower with more than 3,000 labels,

10 Scarpetta
MAP Q2 ■ The Cosmopolitan, 3708 Las Vegas Blvd S. ■ 877 893 2003 ■ Closed daily L ■ $$$
The finest Italian restaurant in Las Vegas, Scarpetta enjoys views of the famous Bellagio fountains. Signature pastas are made in-house daily and are paired with high-quality, locally sourced ingredients.

The elegant decor of the Italian restaurant Scarpetta

For a key to restaurant price ranges see p86

🔟 Vegas Dining Experiences

Open-air dining at Mon Ami Gabi

dinner, why not drop in at one of the very few stand-alone options *(see p103)* on the Strip? This classic, gleaming, all-night burger joint is located directly across from the CityCenter complex.

1 Mon Ami Gabi

The first of its kind in Las Vegas, this open-air Parisian-style brasserie *(see p84)* is still deemed the best, two decades after its launch. Located right next to the Strip, it offers beautifully presented, authentic French classics, from onion soup to steak frites. Their signature rolling wine cart features endless great wines. It is also a good place to enjoy Bellagio's fountain show.

2 House of Blues
MAP R2 ■ Mandalay Pl, 3930 Las Vegas Blvd S. ■ 702 632 7607 ■ www.houseofblues. com/lasvegas

Open daily, the House of Blues has a menu of homemade, Southern-inspired dishes such as New Orleans jambalaya and gumbo, Low-country shrimp and grits, Delta-fried chicken, and a wide range of burgers, sand-wiches, and salads. Live music accompanies the all-you-can-eat Sunday Gospel Brunch.

3 Fatburger
If you are getting tired of casino restaurants, and fancy a taste of what America's really having for

4 Eiffel Tower Restaurant
MAP Q2 ■ Paris, 3655 Las Vegas Blvd S. ■ 702 948 6937 ■ www.eiffeltower restaurant.com ■ $$$

Where else can you dine in style inside the Eiffel Tower, while taking in the wonderful views over a legendary city? Well, in Paris, France, of course – but that doesn't have the spectacle of the Bellagio fountains opposite. Be it *foie gras torchon* with duck prosciutto and fig, or the roasted rack of lamb, the food served here is a feast for both eyes as well as the soul.

5 Triple George Grill
This Downtown steakhouse *(see p94)*, with the feel of an old-time speakeasy, is regularly packed with local lawyers and politicians. The eponymous George, incidentally, is a Las Vegas slang term for a big tipper, and all-round decent guy (as opposed to a "stiff," who never tips, no matter how much they win).

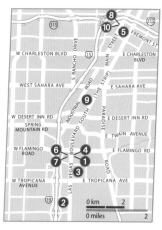

Interior of the Bellagio Patisserie

6 Bellagio Patisserie
MAP Q1–2 ■ Bellagio, 3600 Las Vegas Blvd S. ■ 702 693 8865 ■ www.bellagio.com ■ $

For sheer, mouthwatering spectacle, Las Vegas holds nothing to match the amazing chocolate fountain at this Bellagio bakery. Cascading in enticing coils from ceiling to floor around the entire room, it is the largest one in the world, and lures in customers for crêpes, pastries, and coffee as well as to appreciate the chocolate fountain itself.

7 Pool Café & Bar
MAP Q1–2 ■ 3600 Las Vegas Blvd S. ■ 702 693 8865 ■ www.bellagio.com ■ $$

There are several restaurants at Bellagio that offer the option of alfresco dining, but this is the nicest of the lot to relish a light breakfast or lunch. Enjoy the Swiss-style Bircher muesli, healthy wraps, or a Pacific smoked salmon bagel. Sip on their handcrafted cocktails and refreshing coolers, as you watch the famous fountains at play.

8 Oscar's Steakhouse
This old-fashioned Downtown steakhouse, housed in the strange glass dome of the Plaza (see p93) with views over Fremont Street, is a real only-in-Vegas experience. It is named after Oscar Goodman, the former mayor of the city (and therefore, also lovingly dubbed "Hizzoner"). The hostesses will tell you the history of Las Vegas while you dine.

9 Top of the World
MAP M3 ■ Stratosphere Casino, Hotel & Tower, 2000 Las Vegas Blvd S. ■ 702 380 7711 ■ www.topoftheworldlv.com ■ $$$

Perched at a height of 844 ft (257 m) on the top floor of the Stratosphere, a short distance from the north end of the Strip, this entire dining room rotates every 80 minutes. It is regularly hailed as the most romantic restaurant for dinner in the city, but if you really want to enjoy the views, come at lunchtime.

10 Hash House A Go Go
There are five Hash House A Go Go (see p94) outlets in Las Vegas, but its all-American diner aesthetic. Its menu of "twisted farm food" (healthy country-style classics served in oversize portions) and crafted cocktails make it an especially good fit with Downtown.

Hash House A Go Go's distinctive sign

🔟 Buffets

① Le Village Buffet

MAP Q2 ▪ Paris Las Vegas, 3655 Las Vegas Blvd S. ▪ 702 946 7000 ▪ $$

An innovative blend of offerings at the Paris Las Vegas, including omelets, imported cheeses, bouillabaisse, wild mushroom bisque, lamb, venison, prime rib steak, and huge shrimp, all followed by a wealth of indulgent French-inspired desserts.

② Wicked Spoon

MAP Q2 ▪ The Cosmopolitan, 3708 Las Vegas Blvd S. ▪ 877 893 2001 ▪ $$

Tucked away at the back of The Cosmopolitan's upper level, this bright buffet has quickly established itself as a favorite with lunching locals. Unusually, most dishes are displayed as individual servings, but you can help yourself to however many you want. Brunch here is equally popular.

③ Bacchanal Buffet

MAP P1 ▪ Caesars Palace, 3570 Las Vegas Blvd ▪ 702 731 7928 ▪ $$$

This show-stopping buffet at Caesars Palace offers more than 500 fresh dishes and about 15 chef's specials daily. With its chic, upscale interiors and contemporary food presentation,

the Bacchanal Buffet is worth a visit for its enormous variety of food. Choose from the air, wood, and water-themed sections of the dining rooms. Don't forget to try the fried chicken and waffles, as well as the red velvet pancakes.

④ Bellagio Buffet

MAP Q1–2 ▪ Bellagio, 3600 Las Vegas Blvd S. ▪ 888 987 6667 ▪ $$

A large, sumptuous dining buffet offering more than 60 dishes, ranging from Japanese and Chinese to Italian and new American cuisine. Specialties include all the shrimps you can eat, wild duck breast, and roast venison. Save room for the decadent cheesecake.

The upscale Bacchanal Buffet at Caesars Palace

Elegant Wynn Buffet

5 Wynn Buffet
MAP N2 ■ Wynn Las Vegas, 3131 Las Vegas Blvd S. ■ 702 770 3463 ■ $$

A very strong contender for the best buffet in town, this no-expense-spared extravaganza has the feel of a gourmet restaurant, with individual dishes labeled in appetizing detail. The selection is superb: 16 food kitchens prepare seafood and roast meats. Save room for the sweetshop station and gelato bar.

6 Flavors Buffet
MAP P2 ■ Harrah's, 3475 Las Vegas Blvd S. ■ 702 369 5000 ■ $

The Caesars group of hotels has a reputation for excellent food. Although the buffet offerings at the Flavors Buffet are not as unusual as those of some competitors, the standards of preparation and service are consistently high. Customers in the know go for the salads and extremely attractive desserts.

7 Golden Nugget Buffet
MAP K4 ■ Golden Nugget Hotel, 129 Fremont St ■ 702 386 8152 ■ $

There are around 60 buffet rooms in Las Vegas, and most could not be described as aesthetically lovely. The setting of the Golden Nugget, however, is just that. The dishes are delicious: try the carved turkey and old-fashioned bread pudding.

8 Studio B Buffet
MAP P4 ■ The M Resort, 12300 Las Vegas Blvd S., Henderson ■ 702 797 1880 ■ $

Integrating a top-notch restaurant with live-action cooking, this buffet is unlike any other in Las Vegas. The 600-seat restaurant serves some of the best patisserie desserts, including the popular mini crème brûlée, and numerous chocolate souffles, cookies, and tarts.

9 The Buffet at ARIA
MAP Q1 ■ ARIA, 3730 Las Vegas Blvd S. ■ 702 590 7111 ■ $$

ARIA's bright, stylish dining room doesn't offer quite as many dishes as most, but that's because the chefs concentrate on creating one or two excellent items for each cuisine. The Indian meats and breads, baked in a tandoori oven, are wonderful.

The Buffet at ARIA

10 Carnival World & Seafood Buffet
MAP P1 ■ Rio All-Suite Hotel & Casino, 3700 W. Flamingo Rd ■ 702 777 7757 ■ $$$

The successful Village Seafood Buffet merged with the Carnival World Buffet in November 2015 and continues to be a favorite with local residents. With more than 300 options, fresh crab, shrimp, oysters, and other seafood are flown in daily.

For a key to restaurant price ranges see p86

🔟 Places to Shop

The boutique-lined Via Bellagio

1 Via Bellagio
MAPQ1–2 ■ Bellagio, 3600 Las Vegas Blvd S. ■ www.bellagio.com

Simply walking along Via Bellagio (see p14) is an unforgettable experience. The boutiques are so opulent as to be intimidating: even if you dare not step inside, then at least the entrances to Fendi, Chanel, Gucci, and others are large enough to see inside. Tiffany's windows are especially dazzling during the holiday season.

2 Fashion Show Mall
MAP N2 ■ 3200 Las Vegas Blvd S. ■ www.thefashionshow.com

An upscale shoppers' paradise, Fashion Show Mall boasts Saks Fifth Avenue and Nordstrom department stores. The mall also hosts regular fashion shows and events.

The swanky Crystals at CityCenter

3 Miracle Mile Shops
MAP Q2 ■ Planet Hollywood Resort and Casino, 3667 Las Vegas Blvd S. ■ www.miraclemileshops lv.com

The latest shoe styles at Shoe Palace, leisure wear at Urban Outfitters, and beautiful accessories at Swarovski can be found here. There are more than 200 specialty shops and restaurants, including Club Tattoo, featuring top tattoo artists.

4 The Forum Shops at Caesars Palace
These shops are laid out along pseudo-Roman streets within the Caesars Palace resort complex (see pp20–21), characterized by two-story store-fronts topped with statues of Roman senators. Along with wares from Europe, American design is featured at stores such as Coach, Brighton, and Brooks Brothers. During the holiday season, The Forum Shops are particularly popular. An expansion added a further 175,000 sq ft (16,258 sq m) and additional levels to the complex.

5 Crystals at CityCenter
MAP Q1–2 ■ 3720 Las Vegas Blvd S. ■ www.simon.com/mall/the-shops-at-crystals

Featuring the highest concentration of designer flagship stores in the world, this high-end shopping area lures visitors with retailers including Prada, Gucci, Versace, Hermes, Valentino, Ermenegildo, Sisley, Tom Ford, Tiffany & Co., and Dolce & Gabbana.

6 The Galleria at Sunset
MAP E5 ■ 1300 W. Sunset
Rd, Henderson ■ www.galleriaat
sunset.com

One of the city's residential malls, the Galleria at Sunset offers department store shopping and down-to-earth services, such as jewelry repair, free jewelry cleaning, alterations and tailoring, hairstyling, beauty treatments, and gift wrapping.

7 The Shoppes at Mandalay Place
MAP R1–2 ■ Mandalay Bay,
3950 Las Vegas Blvd S.

An eclectic selection of shops located on a 100,000-sq-ft (9,290-sq-m) sky bridge, Mandalay Place connects The Shoppes at Mandalay Bay with Luxor Hotel and Casino. Stores include Lush, which sells quality handmade cosmetics. There are plenty of restaurants and bars as well, including Minus5° *(see p65)*, one of Las Vegas's ice bars.

8 Town Square Las Vegas
MAP C5 ■ 6605 Las Vegas
Blvd S. ■ www.mytownsquarelas
vegas.com

Take some time out from the Strip's sensory overload at this large outdoor shopping center with its village-like storefronts and quaint streetscapes. The 120-plus stores include big-name favorites such as Abercrombie & Fitch, H&M, and Apple. There is an 18-screen movie theater and a kids' playground, boasting a 42-ft- (13-m-) tall treehouse and 30 pop-jet fountains, along with a GameWorks Entertainment Center that has LAN gaming facilities.

9 The Grand Canal Shoppes at The Venetian
MAP P2 ■ The Venetian, 3355 Las
Vegas Blvd S. ■ www.grandcanal
shoppes.com

Located on the second floor of The Venetian *(see pp16–17)*, the exquisite Grand Canal Shoppes exude European elegance. On offer are handmade Venetian lace, glass, and masks as well as silks, shoes, and jewelry

The Grand Canal Shoppes

from various European countries. Part of the pleasure of shopping here is the ambience – it may not be quite like the real Venice, but the experience is enjoyable.

10 Las Vegas North Premium Outlets
MAP K3 ■ 875 S. Grand Central
Parkway ■ www.premiumoutlets.com

This colossal mall features outlets run by big-name designer brands, such as Adidas and Lacoste, which sell discontinued product lines and factory-line rejects for highly reduced prices. The owners run another mall of the same name on Las Vegas Boulevard south of the Strip, but this one offers more discounts.

⟨TOP 10⟩ Las Vegas for Free

Pete Vallee performing as Big Elvis

1 Big Elvis
MAP P2 ▪ The Piano Bar, Harrah's, 3475 Las Vegas Blvd S. ▪ 702 369 5111 ▪ Open 2–5pm Thu & Fri ▪ www.caesars.com/harrahs-las-vegas/shows/big-elvis

If you are here to see Elvis, then you have come to the right place – the large and highly likable impersonator Pete Vallee puts on a fabulous free show on weekday afternoons, performing the greatest hits of "the king of rock and roll."

2 Fremont Street Experience
Not only have they put a roof over Downtown Las Vegas, but after dark it becomes a vast screen, onto which are projected extravagant nightly light-and-sound shows (see p91). Bands also

The iconic Las Vegas sign

play on street-level stages, and there is no shortage of street performers to add to the entertainment.

3 Wildlife Habitat
Stroll into the tropical gardens of the Flamingo Las Vegas (see p51) and discover the unexpected treat of a lagoon that is also home to a beautiful flock of genuine and

strikingly pink Chilean flamingoes. Pelicans, Ring Teal Ducks, Sacred ibis and tiny hummingbirds can also be seen lurking amid the foliage.

4 Circus Entertainment
Deep in the heart of Circus Circus (see p81), a parade of jugglers, acrobats, clowns, and even stunt bikers lives up to the original theme of the casino when it was first opened in the 1960s. There are free performances every half hour starting from 1:30pm Monday to Thursday and from 11:30am Friday to Sunday.

5 The Mirage Volcano
Crowds of onlookers still gather on the sidewalk of the Strip to admire the nightly pyrotechnics of the famous volcano outside the Mirage (see p83), which first erupted back in 1989. The spectacle now features a thunderous soundtrack by the drummer Mickey Hart from the 1960s rock band the Grateful Dead as well as the Indian *tabla* maestro, Zakir Hussain.

6 The Las Vegas Sign
MAP C5 ▪ 5100 Las Vegas Blvd S. ▪ Open 24hr daily

First unveiled in 1959, this iconic neon sign, situated half a mile (1 km) south of the Michelob ULTRA Arena (see p60), has been listed on the National Register of Historic Places since 2009. Only drivers heading south along the Strip can access it; bring your selfie stick along for a souvenir photo.

7 Fountains of Bellagio
Spouting high, spurting far, swirling sinuously, and swaying seductively, the spectacular displays of the Bellagio fountains (see p81), submerged in the waters of its placid Strip-front lake, are the best-loved free show in all of Las Vegas.

⑧ Million-Dollar Photo
MAP J4 ■ Binions, 128 E. Fremont St ■ 702 382 1600 ■ Open 9am–11:30pm daily ■ www.binions.com

Visitors to Binions casino, situated in Downtown Las Vegas, can pose for souvenir photos with a million dollars in cash. The only catch is that you have to wait half an hour before the print of your photo is ready to be picked up.

⑨ Fall of Atlantis
MAP P1 ■ Forum Shops, 3500 Las Vegas Blvd S. ■ 702 893 3807 ■ Performances on the hour: noon–8pm Thu–Mon ■ www.forum shops.com

With their artificial sky and ancient Roman decor, the Forum Shops make a great free show in their own right, but you can't beat the moment when the animatronic "statues" in its Atlantis fountain spring to life.

⑩ M&M's World
MAP R2 ■ 3785 Las Vegas Blvd S. ■ 702 740 2504 ■ Open 9am–midnight daily ■ www.mmsworld.com

Granted, kids are more likely than adults to thrill at the prospect of this "retail-entertainment attraction" spread over four stories, but surprisingly enough, they're not wrong. It's actually great fun, and includes a free 3D movie starring the M&M characters Red and Yellow.

Entrance to M&M's World

TOP 10 BUDGET TIPS

Visitors gambling in the casino

1 As long as you are gambling, the casino will ply you with free alcoholic drinks – but be sure to tip.

2 For better hotel rates, visit on weekdays – and avoid conventions, holidays, and other important events.

3 Buffets generally offer very good value for money. You will also save money by eating your big meal of the day at lunchtime, when buffets usually cost a few dollars less than at night.

4 Discount tickets for shows are sold online, and at four kiosks on the Strip by Tix4Tonight (*www.tix4 tonight.com*).

5 Register with the "players' clubs" in casinos in order to benefit from assorted discounts.

6 Only rent a car when you actually need it – and when you do, you will get better rates at the airport than from your hotel.

7 Ask about discount coupons in your hotel, and look for more in the free magazines you can pick up from the information center run by the Las Vegas Convention & Visitors Authority (*www.lvcva.com*).

8 Use the city buses, and buy an $8 24-hour pass or a $20 3-day pass. (*www.rtcsnv.com*)

9 Many shows offer two-for-one deals on tickets; ask for these and more at the ticket counters.

10 To save money on entertainment, check out the calendar sections of local papers and magazines, where free events are often listed. Almost every casino lounge puts on free live music to entice people in.

🔟 Festivals and Events

Chinese New Year decorations

1 Chinese New Year
MAP B4 ■ Chinatown Plaza, Spring Mountain Rd ■ Late Jan–mid-Feb

Chinese New Year festivities center on Chinatown Plaza (see p97). Highlights include the traditional Chinese lion dance, Chinese food, firecrackers, and feng shui as it pertains to the New Year.

2 St. Patrick's Day Celebration
MAP K4 ■ Mar 17 or closest weekend

St. Patrick's parties are held at various restaurants and bars, with the main celebration at the Fremont Street Experience (see p91). Crowd-pleasers include a full line-up of music, entertainment, green beer (with green food coloring), and traditional Irish dishes.

3 Cinco de Mayo
All around the city
■ May 5 or closest weekend

The Mexican national holiday, commemorating the victory of the Mexicans over the French in 1862, is celebrated up and down the Strip and around Las Vegas. Traditional Hispanic music is played in performance spaces, margaritas are poured freely, and typical food like tacos and tamales are served at celebration spots around the city.

4 Electric Daisy Carnival
Las Vegas Motor Speedway, 7000 Las Vegas Blvd N. ■ May ■ lasvegas.electricdaisycarnival.com

This three-day electronic dance music festival features art, carnival rides, circus-style performances, and electronic dance music DJs. It has been known to attract more than 30,000 revelers each year.

5 Greek Food Festival
MAP B5 ■ St. John the Baptist Greek Orthodox Church, 5300 S. El Camino Las Vegas ■ 702 221 8245 ■ Sep or Oct ■ www.lvgff.com

Ever since the early 1970s, the Las Vegas Greek Food Festival has celebrated all the aromas, sounds, tastes, and traditions of Greece. The festival runs for four days and includes continuous dancing with live Greek bands, fabulous Greek food, stalls selling artworks and more, as well as a marathon run for charity.

6 Pacific Islands Festival
MAP G6 ■ Henderson Events Plaza, 200 S. Water St ■ 702 267 2171 ■ Sep

The many Pacific Rim peoples who live in the Las Vegas area celebrate their various heritages with traditional entertainment, cultural exhibits, and fashion boutiques. Food includes everything from *kimchi* and *poi* to potstickers and teriyaki.

7 Halloween Haunted Houses
Late Oct ■ www.vegashaunted houses.com

Several companies set up dozens of haunted houses in parking lots, community centers, and parks. Some are heavy on the scare factor while others are more like fun houses, with warped mirrors and a few twisted surprises.

8 Magical Forest

MAP B3 ■ Opportunity Village, 6300 W. Oakey Blvd ■ 702 259 3741 ■ Nov–Jan ■ www.opportunity village.org

Opportunity Village, an organization that helps people with specific needs, raises funds by creating a Magical Forest with hundreds of decorated Christmas trees, holiday lights, and a gingerbread house display. There is nightly entertainment appropriate for all ages, and a fun passenger train.

9 National Finals Parties

Various venues ■ Dec

During the National Finals Rodeo, all of Las Vegas seems to go country – wearing jeans and boots. Casinos bring in country music bands, and line dancing is encouraged. The free entertainment magazines are the best sources of information about what's going on where. The Cowboy Christmas Gift Show is one of the most popular events.

Fireworks on New Year's Eve

10 New Year's Eve

Dec 31

Nowhere celebrates New Year's Eve quite like Las Vegas. The entire city goes into party mode, with big-name headliners performing in the major theaters, and special events in all the nightclubs. Hotel rates, too, are at their highest. At midnight, the Strip's skyline fills with firework displays.

TOP 10 SPORTS EVENTS

Ricky Stenhouse Jr. at NASCAR

1 NASCAR Cup Series
Las Vegas Motor Speedway ■ Mar
Watch Sprint Cup car practices as well as races.

2 Baseball
1650 S. Pavilion Center Dr ■ Apr–Labor Day
Watch the Las Vegas Aviators on their home ground.

3 World Series of Poker
Rio All-Suites Hotel & Casino ■ May–Jul
Poker players compete for millions.

4 Las Vegas Triathlon
Lake Mead ■ Sep
Sprint, Olympic, and half races.

5 NFL Football
Allegiant Stadium, 3333 Al Davis Way, Paradise ■ Sep–Feb
Las Vegas's state-of-the-art Allegiant stadium is home to the Raiders and hosts several games during NFL season.

6 Shriners Hospitals for Children Open
TPC Summerlin ■ Oct
Attracts PGA golfers for a good cause.

7 PBR Championship
T-Mobile Arena ■ Oct or Nov
Professional bull-riding competition.

8 National Finals Rodeo
Thomas & Mack Center ■ Early Dec
Cowboys compete for million-dollar prizes at the USA's premier rodeo.

9 World Championship Boxing
Caesars Palace, MGM Grand, Mandalay Bay, T-Mobile Arena, Thomas & Mack Center
Las Vegas is still the premier city for big-name title bouts.

10 NHRA Summit Nationals
Las Vegas Motor Speedway, 7000 Las Vegas Blvd N. ■ Dates vary
Dragsters battle for supremacy.

Las Vegas
Area by Area

View across the Fountains of Bellagio to
the Caesars Palace Las Vegas Hotel and Casino

🔟 The Strip

Walk along the Strip and you'll see that some of the best things in Las Vegas life are free – especially when it comes to sightseeing and entertainment. It costs nothing to walk through the hotel-casinos, and you can window-shop to your heart's content in their shopping promenades. The hotels' architecture makes for an attraction in its own right: where else would you find an Egyptian sphinx, the Eiffel Tower, Venetian canals, and a medieval castle on the same street? In addition, some hotel-casinos have free entertainment going on outside their doors.

Flamingo Wildlife Habitat

THE STRIP

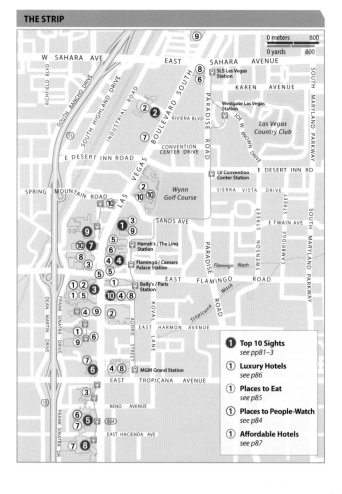

1 Top 10 Sights
see pp81–3

1 Luxury Hotels
see p86

1 Places to Eat
see p85

1 Places to People-Watch
see p84

1 Affordable Hotels
see p87

Gondolas at The Venetian

1 The Venetian

Sheldon Adelson, the late owner of the largest hotel-casino on the Strip, enjoyed his honeymoon in Venice, Italy, so much that he brought the entire city home with him. At least, that's how it looks – as well as its showpiece Grand Canal, complete with singing gondoliers, The Venetian *(see pp16–17)* includes replicas of landmarks, such as the Rialto Bridge, St. Mark's Square, and the Doge's Palace. Simply stroll in off the Strip and you can admire its art and architecture for free; its 7,000-plus hotel rooms, and its restaurants, nightclubs, and shops, cost a little more, of course.

2 Circus Circus

Performances every half hour: 1:30pm–midnight Mon–Thu, 11:30am–midnight Fri–Sun

Over the course of more than 40 years, Circus Circus *(see p87)* has entertained hundreds of thousands of spectators with its impressive shows. Stars have included the Flying Farfans of Argentina and the miniature-bicycle rider Charles Charles of Paris. With performances taking place every half hour, you can pop back for different shows and catch a wide variety of acts.

3 Fountains of Bellagio

Performance times vary across seasons, check website: www.bellagio.mgmresorts.com

More than 1,000 fountains perform a water ballet above Lake Bellagio, in defiance of the parched, baking desert that surrounds the city. Soaring as high as 240 ft (73 m) in the air, the cascading water is choreographed to classical music. Bellagio and the other properties in the MGM Mirage group use incandescent lighting rather than neon, which makes the lit-up Italian village surrounding the lake a lovely backdrop for the dancing waters *(see p86)*.

4 Flamingo Wildlife Habitat

Open 24hr daily

The 15-acre (6-ha) habitat at Flamingo Las Vegas, improbably located in the heart of the Las Vegas Strip, is home to 70 birds, including Chilean flamingoes, pelicans, and black swans, more than 300 fish, and 30 turtles. It is a welcome oasis in the often overwhelming desert environment *(see p87)*.

5 Luxor

A strikingly modern twist on an ancient classic, the unique 30-floor, black-glass pyramid of the Luxor *(see p40)* is one of the most recognizable landmarks in Las Vegas. The structure is topped with a 42.3-billion candela (315,000-watt) light beam, a Vegas icon, which is visible from space and is the strongest beam of light in the world. The hotel-casino's awe-inspiring atrium, at 29 million cubic ft (820,000 cubic m), is one of the largest in the world. A mighty 10-story sphinx (larger than the Egyptian original) guards the premises. Luxor is also home to a Blue Man Group stage production, *Criss Angel Mindfreak Live!*, *Titanic: The Artifact Exhibition*, and *Bodies... The Exhibition*.

Luxor's pyramid and sphinx

The New York-New York hotel-casino complex

6 New York-New York

More manageable in scale than most of the Strip giants, while still featuring facsimiles of everything from the Brooklyn Bridge to the Empire State Building, this endearing microcosm *(see p41)* of Manhattan is irresistible, both inside and out. Most of its replica buildings are approximately half life-size; amazingly, though, the Statue of Liberty stands twice as high as the original. Thrill-seekers can circle the whole lot in the tiny yellow cabs of the Big Apple Roller Coaster.

7 The Forum Shops at Caesars Palace

Use the first spiral-shaped escalator of its kind in the United States to reach the shopping destinations of your choice, or ride it just for fun *(see pp20–21)*. In the Roman Great Hall, check out the 50,000-gallon (189,304-liter) saltwater aquarium, home to hundreds of colorful tropical fish. Keep an eye out for the spectacle of divers feeding the fish, which happens twice a day, usually in the afternoon. Some of the shops provide entertainment, but often the most fun can be had by taking a break on a bench to watch shoppers from all around the world.

8 Shark Reef Aquarium at Mandalay Bay

Open 10am–6pm daily; summer: 10am–10pm daily ▪ Adm

It is truly awe-inspiring to wander within the special walkways of the 1.3-million-gallon (4.9-million-liter) aquarium and observe the thousands of wonderful sea creatures swimming together. Look out for the arowana dragon fish – and, of course, 15 different species of shark *(see p50)*.

AN EXPANDING CITY

Las Vegas saw rapid expansion through construction of hotels, condominiums, and shopping facilities before an economic decline hit the city in the mid-2000s. Many projects were put on hold or abandoned. Today, it's growing again, with several exciting projects, such as the opening of Virgin Hotels Las Vegas and Resorts World in 2021 and the MSG Sphere, due to open in 2023.

⑨ The Mirage Volcano
Erupts daily: 7pm, 8pm, 9pm, 10pm & 11pm ■ www.mirage.com/en/amenities/volcano.html

With displays like this, it is hardly surprising that the Mirage, when it was opened in 1989, is said to have triggered the 1990s hotel-building boom. The artificial, multimillion-dollar volcano *(see p86)* spews fire 100 ft (30 m) into the air every night. Ingenious lighting and steam effects convey the drama of lava flows, while loudspeakers broadcast vivid sound effects featuring the work of Grateful Dead drummer Mickey Hart and Indian *tabla* sensation Zakir Hussain.

The Mirage Volcano

⑩ Paris Las Vegas
The iconic Eiffel Tower and Arc de Triomphe are faithfully and impressively reproduced at Paris Las Vegas *(see p86)*, albeit on a smaller scale than the originals. You can buy fresh baguettes from a "street vendor," and nibble it to the strains of tunes by the great Maurice Chevalier, as interpreted by a wandering accordion player. The tower's glass elevator promises spectacular views from the top.

Paris Las Vegas

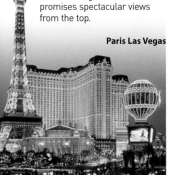

A DAY ON THE STRIP

▶ **MORNING**

Start at **Mandalay Bay**, be sure to visit the crocodiles in Shark Reef Aquarium. Head north along the Strip, taking in the multicolored turrets of **Excalibur** *(see p87)* and the mighty pyramid and sphinx of **Luxor** *(see p81)*. Then stop by the Il Fornaio bakery in **New York-New York**.

Then head up further north – it's quite a hike, so you may opt to take the Deuce bus *(see p124)* – to the **Flamingo Wildlife Habitat** *(see p81)*. Now cross over to the Roman extravaganza of Caesars Palace, for lunch in the **Bacchanal Buffet** *(see p70)*.

AFTERNOON

At the **Forum Shops** at **Caesars Palace** you may well shed the shoppers in your party.

Next stop is **The Venetian** *(see p81)*, to be serenaded by operatic gondoliers on the Grand Canal, and enjoy a genuine Italian gelato in St. Mark's Square.

Another walk or bus ride will take you to **Circus Circus** *(see p81)* to catch free of cost circus acts on the Midway or venture into the thrilling rides in the Adventuredome.

Once the sun goes down, savor two of the Strip's finest free spectacles. First watch **The Mirage Volcano** erupt, then continue to **Paris Las Vegas**, where excellent restaurants, including one within the replica Eiffel Tower, offer great views of the **Fountains of Bellagio** *(see p81)*.

See map on p80 ←

Places to People-Watch

① Bellagio Lobby
MAP Q1–2 ▪ Bellagio,
3600 Las Vegas Blvd S.

Settle down on a sofa to watch the fashionable jet set coming and going. Relax with piano music from the caviar bar, Petrossian, and admire the marvelous artistry of the ceiling.

② Fountains at Miracle Mile Shops
MAP Q2 ▪ Planet Hollywood,
3667 Las Vegas Blvd S.

When shopping gets tiring, sit down near the fountain in the heart of the Miracle Mile Shops at Planet Hollywood, and watch the illuminated fountain show set to original music.

③ Around the Casino Tables
The stars play at upscale casinos such as the MGM Grand, The Cosmopolitan, Bellagio, and Caesars Palace; stargazers should aim, apparently, for 11pm to 1am on weekends.

④ The Forum Shops at Caesars Palace
MAP P1–2 ▪ Caesars, 3570
Las Vegas Blvd S.

The cafés and benches within the shopping complex (see pp20–21) are as good for taking a break as they are for people-watching.

⑤ Footbridges along the Strip
MAP N–R2

Hop across Las Vegas Boulevard without playing traffic roulette, and enjoy marvelous vantage points of the thronging mêlée below.

⑥ Bodies... The Exhibition
MAP R1 ▪ Luxor Hotel & Casino, 3900 Las Vegas Blvd S.

Explore the beauty of the human body. This exhibit at Luxor (see p81) gives visitors a whole new perspective of the anatomy of human beings, inside out.

⑦ The Park
MAP Q1 ▪ 3782 Las Vegas Blvd S.

With its numerous restaurants, bars, and entertainment venues, The Park is a great place to enjoy a meal or a concert, or to simply spend time people-watching.

⑧ Fiber-Optic Signs
MAP R2 ▪ MGM Grand,
3799 Las Vegas Blvd S.

An increasing number of supersize signs like the one at MGM are appearing on the Strip. Expect to see vivid, lifelike clips of performers and upcoming attractions.

⑨ Third Floor of The Cosmopolitan
MAP Q1–2 ▪ 3708 Las Vegas Blvd S.

Take a seat in one of the comfy chairs near the pool table and watch people as they come and go from the resort's restaurants.

⑩ Mon Ami Gabi
MAP Q2 ▪ Paris Las Vegas Hotel, 3655 Las Vegas Blvd S. ▪ 702 944 4224 ▪ $$

Take a table at the sidewalk café, soak up the atmosphere, and enjoy the view of Bellagio's fountain show.

The Forum Shops at Caesars Palace

Places to Eat

Interiors of Picasso restaurant

1 Picasso
MAP Q1–2 ▪ Bellagio, 3600 Las Vegas Blvd S. ▪ 702 693 8865 ▪ Open 5:30–10pm Wed–Sun ▪ $$$

The menu's (see p66) modern cuisine is inspired by the regional dishes of France and Spain, where renowned artist Pablo Picasso lived.

2 La Cave
MAP N2 ▪ Wynn Las Vegas, 3131 Las Vegas Blvd S. ▪ 702 770 7375 ▪ Open 4–9pm daily (to 10pm Fri & Sat), brunch Sat & Sun ▪ $$$

Chef Billy DeMarco's dishes are paired with artisanal draught beers and an exceptional wine list.

3 Bouchon
MAP P2 ▪ The Venetian, 3355 Las Vegas Blvd ▪ 702 414 6200 ▪ Open 8am–1pm & 5–10pm daily ▪ $$$

Classical French-bistro cuisine prepared using the season's finest ingredients is served in this casual yet elegant dining room (see p67).

4 L'Atelier de Joël Robuchon
MAP R2 ▪ MGM Grand, 3799 ▪ Las Vegas Blvd S. ▪ 702 891 7925 ▪ $$$

The chefs here create exquisite French-inspired tapas and tasting menus in an open kitchen (see p66).

5 Michael Mina
MAP Q1–2 ▪ Bellagio, 3600 Las Vegas Blvd S. ▪ 702 693 7223 ▪ Open 5–10pm Wed–Sun ▪ $$$

The fusion of Japanese and French flavors is integral to Mina's cuisine.

6 Bazaar Meat by José Andrés
MAP M3 ▪ Sahara, 2535 Las Vegas Blvd S. ▪ 702 761 7000 ▪ Open 5–10pm Wed–Sun ▪ $$$

Award-winning, Michelin-starred chef José Andrés celebrates meat dishes at this stunning steakhouse.

7 Border Grill
MAP R1 ▪ Mandalay Bay, 3950 Las Vegas Blvd S. ▪ 702 632 7403 ▪ Open 11am–10pm (from 10am Sat & Sun) ▪ $$

Chefs Mary Sue Milliken and Susan Feniger, stars of Food Network's *Too Hot Tamales*, present Mexican cuisine.

8 Restaurant Guy Savoy
MAP P1–2 ▪ Caesars Palace, 3570 Las Vegas Blvd S. ▪ 702 731 7286 ▪ Open 5:30–9:30pm Wed–Sun; closed mid-Jul–mid-Aug ▪ $$$

Celebrated chef Guy Savoy's New French cuisine is prepared with the finest ingredients.

9 CATCH
MAP P1–2 ▪ ARIA, 3730 Las Vegas Blvd S. ▪ 702 590 5757 ▪ Open 5–10:30pm daily, also 10am–2pm Sat & Sun ▪ $$$

This fine-dining restaurant offers sushi, steak, and seafood, with fresh fish flown in daily.

10 SW Steakhouse
MAP N2 ▪ Wynn Las Vegas, 3131 Las Vegas Blvd S. ▪ 702 770 3325 ▪ Open 5:30–10pm (to 10:30pm Fri & Sat) daily ▪ $$$

Outstanding Kobe beef steaks, seafood and vegan entrées, are flawlessly served in the dining room or on the patio facing the Lake of Dreams.

See map on p80 ←

Luxury Hotels

1 ARIA Resort and Casino
MAP Q1 ▪ 3730 Las Vegas Blvd S. ▪ 702 590 7111 ▪ www.aria.com ▪ $$$

As befits its location, this sleek CityCenter option is more of an upscale business hotel than a showpiece casino.

2 Bellagio
MAP Q1–2 ▪ 3600 Las Vegas Blvd S. ▪ 702 693 7111 ▪ www.bellagio.com ▪ $$$

Opulent Italianate hotel, with luxurious rooms curving around a gleaming lake, and an extravagant pool complex (see pp14–15).

Lobby of Caesars Palace

3 Caesars Palace
MAP P1 ▪ 3570 Las Vegas Blvd S. ▪ 866 227 2938 ▪ www.caesarspalace.com ▪ $$$

The rooms in this Roman palace – Vegas's definitive themed hotel – are more comfortable than ever.

4 The Cosmopolitan
MAP Q2 ▪ 3708 Las Vegas Blvd S. ▪ 702 698 7000 ▪ www.cosmopolitanlasvegas.com ▪ $$$

Large, very comfortable rooms with stylish modern furnishings; many have balconies overlooking the Bellagio fountains.

PRICE CATEGORIES

For a standard, double room per night (with breakfast if included), taxes, and extra charges.

$ under $100 $$ $100–200 $$$ over $200

---

5 The Cromwell
MAP P2 ▪ 3595 Las Vegas Blvd S. ▪ 702 777 3777 ▪ www.thecromwell.com ▪ $$$

The Strip's only "boutique hotel" offers 188 luxuriously appointed rooms.

6 Waldorf Astoria
MAP Q1 ▪ 3752 Las Vegas Blvd S. ▪ 702 590 8888 ▪ www.waldorfastorialasvegas.com ▪ $$$

A stylish, non-gaming hotel situated at the heart of the Strip (see p25), the former Mandarin Oriental is chic.

7 Resorts World
MAP N2 ▪ 3000 Las Vegas Blvd S. ▪ 702 676 7000 ▪ www.rwlasvegas.com ▪ $$$

This 59-story resort, with 3,500 ultra high-tech rooms, is the largest Hilton hotel property in the world.

8 Paris Las Vegas
MAP Q2 ▪ 3655 Las Vegas Blvd S. ▪ 877 796 2096 ▪ www.parislasvegas.com ▪ $$

Well-equipped central hotel, with plush rooms overlooking the Eiffel Tower and the Bellagio fountains.

9 The Venetian
MAP P2 ▪ 3355 Las Vegas Blvd S. ▪ 702 414 1000 ▪ www.venetian.com ▪ $$$

One of the world's largest hotels, the all-suite Venetian (see pp16–17) maintains consistently high standards.

10 Wynn Las Vegas
MAP N2 ▪ 3131 Las Vegas Blvd S. ▪ 702 770 7000 ▪ www.wynnlasvegas.com ▪ $$$

This mega resort (see pp18–19) is the last word in Las Vegas luxury, with large and tasteful rooms.

Affordable Hotels

① Bally's
MAP Q2 ■ 3645 Las Vegas
Blvd S. ■ 877 603 4390 ■ www.
ballyslasvegas.com ■ $

Spacious, good-value rooms in
a very central location, sharing
access to the amenities of the
fancier Paris Las Vegas next door.

② Circus Circus
MAP M–N2 ■ 2880 Las Vegas
Blvd S. ■ 702 734 0410 ■ www.circus
circus.com ■ $

This vast property, crammed with
child-friendly attractions, offers
rock-bottom rates and has
the only RV park on the Strip.

③ Excalibur
MAP R1 ■ 3850 Las Vegas
Blvd S. ■ 702 597 7777 ■ www.
excalibur.com ■ $$

A longtime favorite with budget-
conscious families and tour groups,
this child's-drawing castle has some
surprisingly pleasant rooms.

④ The Flamingo
MAP P2 ■ 3555 Las Vegas
Blvd S. ■ 702 733 3111 ■ www.
flamingolasvegas.com ■ $$

The oldest of the Strip's legendary
casinos is now a mid-range property
that offers some great rates.

⑤ Harrah's
MAP P2 ■ 3475 Las Vegas
Blvd S. ■ 800 214 9110 ■ www.
harrahsvegas.com ■ $

Friendly hotel with comfortable rooms,
in the heart of the Vegas Strip.

Bedroom in The LINQ

⑥ The LINQ
MAP P2 ■ 3535 Las Vegas Blvd
S. ■ 800 634 6441 ■ www.caesars.
com/linq ■ $

The centerpiece of an entertainment
district, The LINQ is one of the Strip's
best bargains and hosts Jimmy
Kimmel's comedy club.

⑦ Luxor
MAP R1 ■ 3900 Las Vegas Blvd S.
■ 702 262 4000 ■ www.luxor.com ■ $

Only in Las Vegas can you sleep in
a glass-walled room in a 30-story
pyramid overlooking a giant sphinx.

⑧ Sahara Las Vegas
MAP M3 ■ 2535 Las Vegas Blvd
S. ■ 702 761 7000 ■ www.saharalas
vegas.com ■ $

The former SLS Las Vegas, now a
mid-range hotel, is well positioned
for Downtown as well as the Strip.

⑨ The Stratosphere
MAP M3 ■ 2000 Las Vegas
Blvd S. ■ 702 380 7777 ■ www.
stratospherehotel.com ■ $

Though the rooms aren't in
its 1,000-ft (304-m) tower, the
Stratosphere offers excellent value.
For a great view with an adrenaline
rush, take a ride to the top.

⑩ TI (Treasure Island)
MAP N2 ■ 3300 Las Vegas
Blvd S. ■ 702 894 7111 ■ www.
treasureisland.com ■ $

Treasure Island has abandoned
its old pirate theme, and now caters
to price-conscious visitors.

Exterior of Harrah's

See map on p80

🔟 Downtown

Downtown Las Vegas is not a place of multi-story financial temples as is the case in most US cities. Instead, it is a conglomeration of government buildings, carnival attractions, not-so-very-glamorous casinos, and shops dealing in souvenirs and unclaimed pawn-shop miscellany. The heart of the area – the pedestrianized and LED-canopied Fremont Street – has a neon-lit row of iconic casinos, bars, restaurants, and, since the mid-1990s, free nightly entertainment in the form of a dazzling light-and-sound show, the Fremont Street Experience. This nightlife zone is here to stay, but a large-scale revitalization has also turned Downtown Las Vegas into a growing center for the arts and culture.

Stratosphere Tower

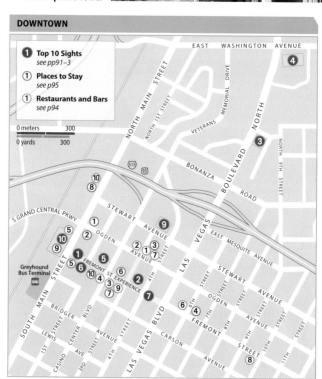

DOWNTOWN

1 Top 10 Sights
see pp91–3

① Places to Stay
see p95

① Restaurants and Bars
see p94

0 meters   300
0 yards   300

Previous pages Nightlife at the Fremont Street Promenade

1 Downtown's Neon Lights

This area *(see pp22–3)* encompasses about eight blocks that front on Fremont Street, between Main and Fourth streets. Along this stretch is the most concentrated dazzle of neon on the planet. Not only are all the Fremont Street casino fronts decorated with neon, but the street signs and light shows above also contribute to the sparkling brilliance. Nighttime, of course, is when the lighting is at its most intense. The crowds on the malled walkway are heavy until after midnight, and the entertainment adds to a feeling of carnival.

2 Fremont Street Experience

MAP K4 ■ Fremont St between Main and 4th

The Fremont Street Experience *(see p22)* encompasses a 1,500 ft (457 m) long LED display canopy, zip lines that are strung beneath the screen, and a pedestrian promenade. It comes alive at night with light-and-sound shows, and live entertainment. Special events take place throughout the year, such as the St. Patrick's Day Celebration in March, Pride Parade in September, and a Veterans Day Parade in November.

LED canopy over Fremont Street

Neon signs at the Neon Museum

3 Neon Museum

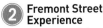
MAP K4 ■ 770 Las Vegas Blvd S. ■ 702 387 6366 ■ Tours only ■ Adm ■ www.neonmuseum.org

Although the very name of Las Vegas remains synonymous with glowing neon, many of the city's finest signs have vanished from its streets. The mission of the Neon Museum is to gather them up and preserve them. Take a tour of its "Boneyard" to see neon gems from the long-lost Silver Slipper and other legendary casinos.

4 Old Las Vegas Mormon Fort Historic State Park

MAP J5 ■ 500 Washington Ave E. ■ 702 486 3511 ■ Open 8am–4:30pm Tue–Sat ■ Adm

Mormons built this fort, along with a trading post in 1855, as a defense against the Paiute peoples (who in fact were peaceful). It is the oldest building of its type in Nevada, but of the original structures, only a small adobe building, which formed part of the stockade, now remains.

5 Downtown Casinos

Along with all the outdoor activity on Fremont Street, there's action inside the casinos, too. They may not be as glamorous as the big hotels on the Strip, but the Fremont Street and other Downtown clubs have more history – some date back to the 1940s. They are also known for their bargain meals and buffets.

NEW YEAR'S EVE IN DOWNTOWN LAS VEGAS

Historically, Downtown has been the place favored by Las Vegas resident revelers for New Year's Eve. Each year since the advent of the Fremont Street Experience, the celebrations have become more elaborate with live music and other entertainment; food and beverages; a countdown to midnight; fireworks (**below**); and dancing in the streets. Of course, there are paper hats and noisemakers, too. However, unlike most Fremont Street happenings on all other days of the year, some of the New Year's Eve festivities are not free.

daredevil riders can choose to be launched along one of two separate zip lines. The lower line consists of ski-lift-style chairs; on the higher line, you're strapped into a harness and fly headfirst above the revelers below along the entire length of the Fremont Street Experience.

8 Street Festivals
MAP K4 ▪ First Fri, throughout Downtown

Downtown Las Vegas's growth and revitalization has resulted in a number of street festivals. In the Arts District, First Friday invites people to explore the galleries and meet the artists. Some of the popular street festivals held are the Great Vegas Festival of Beer in April and the Life is Beautiful festival of music, art, and food, held every September or October.

9 The Mob Museum
MAP J4 ▪ 300 Stewart Ave ▪ 702 229 2734 ▪ Open 9am–9pm daily ▪ Adm ▪ www.themob museum.org

6 Vegas Vic Sign
MAP K4
▪ 25 Fremont St

Erected in 1951, the 40-ft- (12-m-) tall Vegas Vic is a survivor from the early casino days. In bygone times, not only did he smoke and wave but he also talked, saying "Howdy pardner, welcome to Las Vegas." Vic has now become a Las Vegas icon and the backdrop for thousands of visitors' photographs each year.

7 SlotZilla Zip Line
MAP K4 ▪ Fremont St ▪ 702 678 5780 ▪ Open 4pm–1am Mon–Wed, noon–2am Thu–Sun ▪ Adm ▪ www. vegasexperience.com

From what is said to be the world's tallest slot machine, soaring high over Fremont Street,

Vegas's notorious history is on display at the old courthouse, one of the most historic buildings in town. In addition to exhibits specific to Las Vegas, the museum examines organized crime on a larger scale, with artifacts and true-life accounts. A number of weapons, wire-tapping tools, and crime scene photos are displayed side by side with insider accounts on some of the biggest names of organized crime from Al Capone to Whitey Bulger. The museum also examines popular Mob myths, and explains what happens when notable figures retire, die, or go into the witness protection

Vegas Vic Sign

Exhibit at The Mob Museum

program. A distillery, bar, and an interactive Crime Lab are recent additions.

⑩ Plaza Hotel and Casino
MAP J4 ▪ 1 Main St ▪ 702 386 2110 ▪ www.plazahotelcasino.com

From Main Street, the Plaza may look like just another casino, but it sits on a historic spot. Built during the 1970s, the Plaza is located on the very site of the birthplace of Las Vegas, at the first Union Pacific Railroad Depot Station. The station is no longer there, but the original railroad tracks can still be seen on the back side of the property. Three 21-story-tall murals adorn the hotel's Y-shaped walls. It has the only bingo room in Downtown Las Vegas and a session is held every two hours from 11am to 9pm.

Plaza Hotel and Casino

DOWNTOWN AFTER DARK

▶ **LATE AFTERNOON**

Begin your excursion in the mid-to late afternoon, with a visit to the **Neon Museum** to see some iconic Las Vegas signs (see p91). Make sure you have booked yourself onto a tour.

Next, explore Las Vegas's history with a visit to **The Mob Museum**, which offers a peek into the criminal past of the city.

For a special treat, try dining at one of the top restaurants in Downtown, such as Vic & Anthony's Steakhouse at the **Golden Nugget Casino** (see p94), with its classy decor, or the romantic Hugo's Cellar at **Four Queens** (see p94).

NIGHTTIME

After dinner, stroll along Fremont Street's pedestrian promenade, stopping to watch people on the zip lines overhead and the buskers performing on the street. If gaming's your pleasure, step inside the **El Cortez Hotel's** casino for vintage slots (see p95).

Check out the casino at the **Plaza**, then wander down to Main Street Station. Pick up a brochure here with a map and list of treasures – including street lamps from Brussels and a portion of the Berlin Wall – that have been incorporated into the building's interesting decor.

Back at **Fremont Street Experience** (see p91), top off the night by watching the stunning light-and-sound show.

See map on p90 ←

Restaurants and Bars

PRICE CATEGORIES

For a three-course meal for one with half a bottle of wine (or equivalent meal), taxes, and extra charges.

$ under $30 $$ $30–60 $$$ over $60

1 Freedom Beat
MAP J4 ■ Downtown Grand, 206 N. Third St ■ 702 719 5315 ■ www.downtowngrand.com ■ $

Created by chef Scott Commings, the menu takes diners on a culinary trip from Wisconsin to Texas to Colorado.

2 Triple George Grill
MAP J4 ■ 201 N. Third St ■ 702 384 2761 ■ Open 11am–11pm Mon–Sat (to midnight Fri & Sat) ■ www.triplegeorgegrill.com ■ $$

Longstanding steakhouse (see p68) with a rustic vibe favoured by city bigwigs for its power lunch specials.

3 Hugo's Cellar
MAP K4 ■ Four Queens, 202 E. Fremont St ■ 702 385 4011 ■ Open 5–10pm daily ■ www.fourqueens.com ■ $$$

Atomic Liquors

Much-loved on the Downtown dining scene, Hugo's offers a classic menu of rich meat and seafood dishes.

4 Vic & Anthony's Steakhouse
MAP K4 ■ Golden Nugget, 129 E. Fremont St ■ 702 386 8399 ■ www.vicandanthonys.com ■ $$$

A quaint steakhouse in Downtown's fanciest casino serving expensive but delicious prime cuts of beef and veal.

5 Oscar's Steakhouse
MAP J4 ■ The Plaza, 1 Main St ■ 702 386 7227 ■ Open 4–10pm Sun–Thu (to 10:30pm Fri & Sat) ■ www.oscarslv.com ■ $$$

This place (see p69) offers vast views down neon-lit Fairmont St. Plus the dishes here earn rave reviews.

6 Eureka!
MAP K4 ■ 520 E. Fremont St ■ 702 570 3660 ■ Open 11am–midnight Mon–Thu, 10am–midnight Sun (to 1am Fri–Sat) ■ www.eurekarestaurantgroup.com

Located at the eastern edge of the Fremont Street Experience, this bar-restaurant serves gourmet burgers and sandwiches paired with American craft beers, whiskeys, and cocktails.

7 Furnace Bar
MAP J4 ■ Downtown Grand, 206 N. Third St ■ 702 719 5100 ■ www.downtowngrand.com ■ $

Comfortable bar just off the hotel lobby, decorated with crystal chandeliers and ideal for an early-evening cocktail before hitting the casinos.

8 Atomic Liquors
MAP K5 ■ 917 Fremont St ■ 702 982 3000 ■ Opening times vary ■ www.atomic.vegas

Established in 1952, the city's oldest free-standing bar, where rooftop drinkers once watched distant atomic tests, has been meticulously restored.

9 Hash House A Go Go
MAP J4 ■ The Plaza, 1 Main St ■ 702 386 4646 ■ Open 7am–1pm Sun–Thu (to 9pm Fri & Sat) ■ www.hashhouseagogo.com ■ $$

Classic diner (see p69) serving huge portions of popular all-American fare, from pancakes to burgers.

10 Triple Seven Restaurant and Microbrewery
MAP J4 ■ Main Street Station, 200 N. Main St ■ 702 387 1896 ■ Open 5pm–midnight Thu–Mon ■ www.mainstreetcasino.com ■ $

Huge pub/restaurant serving pizzas, gourmet burgers, and sandwiches, along with its selection of superb house-brewed beers.

Places to Stay

PRICE CATEGORIES
For a standard double room per night
(with breakfast if included), including
taxes, and extra charges.
....
$ under $100 $$ $100–200 $$$ over $200

1 California Hotel
MAP J4 ■ 12 Ogden Ave E.
■ 702 385 1222 ■ www.thecal.com ■ $
Just off Fremont St, this small
casino offers plain, good-value
rooms, plus, assorted Hawaiian
restaurants and bars.

2 Circa Resort & Casino
MAP D3 ■ 8 Fremont St
■ 702 247 2258 ■ www.circalas
vegas.com ■ $$$
With more than 700 elegant rooms,
five fabulous restaurants, a huge
pool, and the world's largest Sports
Book, this adults-only hotel provides
a lavish experience.

3 Downtown Grand
MAP J4 ■ 206 N. Third St
■ 702 719 5100 ■ www.downtown
grand.com ■ $
The plush contemporary rooms and
suites in Downtown's newest hotel,
facing the Mob Museum two blocks
from Fremont St, are the best option
for business travelers.

4 El Cortez
MAP K4 ■ 600 E. Fremont St
■ 702 385 5200 ■ www.elcortezhotel
casino.com ■ $
Long a byword for budget accom-
modation, El Cortez is a real
throwback to vintage Vegas, with
some attractive suites as well as
rock-bottom standard rooms.

5 Golden Gate
MAP J4 ■ 1 E. Fremont St
■ 702 385 1906 ■ www.goldengate
casino.com ■ $
The oldest hotel in Las Vegas, founded
across from the railroad station in
1906, is now a self-styled "boutique
hotel" with small but quirky rooms.

6 The Fremont Hotel
MAP K4 ■ 200 E. Fremont St
■ 702 385 3232 ■ www.fremont
casino.com ■ $
One of Downtown's classier options,
in the heart of the Fremont Street
Experience, with attractive rooms.

7 Four Queens
MAP K4 ■ 202 E. Fremont
St ■ 702 385 4011 ■ www.four
queens.com ■ $
Old-fashioned Downtown casino,
where rather ordinary motel-style
rooms are available at bargain rates.

8 Main Street Station
MAP J4 ■ 200 N. Main St
■ 702 387 1896 ■ www.mainstreet
casino.com ■ $
Good-value casino/hotel, close to
Fremont St, with decor designed
to evoke New Orleans in the 1890s.

9 The Plaza
MAP J4 ■ 1 Main St ■ 702
386 2110 ■ www.plazahotelcasino.
com ■ $
Large hotel in the long-defunct rail
station, with some of Downtown's
hippest bars and restaurants.

10 Golden Nugget
MAP K4 ■ 129 E. Fremont
St ■ 702 385 7111 ■ www.golden
nugget.com ■ $$
The only Downtown hotel that
matches the Strip for luxury and
amenities is a self-contained resort,
with a spectacular outdoor pool.

Luxury pool and bar at Golden Nugget

See map on p90

TOP 10 Beyond the Neon

Look beyond the neon and you will find that Las Vegas is, like the Roman god Janus, a two-faced town. One is about make-up and make-believe; the other is like that of other American towns, with popular city parks, a thriving university, community centers, and playgrounds. Las Vegas is a city where significant research is undertaken at medical centers, and where cultural performances take place almost every night. It is also a growing city of surprising diversity, with varied neighborhoods and distinct areas.

UNLV Campus

BEYOND THE NEON

① Chinatown Plaza
MAP B–C4 ■ 4255 Spring
Mountain Rd ■ www.lvchinatown
plaza.com

With pagoda-style roofs, a traditional
Chinese entrance gate, and a statue
of the mythical monk Tripitaka, with
his companions – a pig, a soldier, and
a monkey – Chinatown Plaza is a
shopping strip offering many stores
and restaurants that celebrate
Asian cultures. Chinese music wafts
through the covered walkways, and
art all through the Plaza spotlights
Chinese customs and traditions. Not
surprisingly, this is the place to come
for the best Asian cuisine in town.
There are a number of Filipino,
Korean, Japanese, and Vietnamese
restaurants, in addition to the
Chinese establishments.

Chinatown Plaza

② Broadacres Marketplace & Event Center
MAP D2 ■ 2390 Las Vegas Blvd N.

This swap meet brings together more
than 1,150 vendors selling antiques,
toys, crafts, shoes, and electronics.
Although most items are priced, feel
free to bargain for a better deal. On
weekends, live bands play on a large
stage with a covered seating area.
The food options are plentiful, with
stalls selling everything from
burritos to barbecue fare.

③ UNLV Campus
MAP Q4 ■ S. Maryland Pkwy

City residents' favorite areas for
taking a walk include the campus of
the University of Nevada Las Vegas,
which was established in 1957. The
university may not have any remarkable buildings, but there are shady
trees, and in early evening the paths
are blissfully uncrowded. Be sure not
to miss the lovely desert garden.
Summer days are much warmer
than winter days, but the campus
is less crowded in the summer.

④ Dig This
MAP N1 ■ 800 W Roban Ave
■ 702 222 4344

For those who have always
wanted to experience working in
construction, this heavy equipment
playground is a dream come true.
Choose a bulldozer or excavator,
go through an orientation exercise,
then participate in activities such
as building mounds, stacking tires,
and digging deep trenches. Book in
advance. Visitors must be over 8 years
old and at least 48 in (122 cm) tall.

Ethel M Chocolate Factory

MAP E5 ▪ 2 Cactus Garden Drive, Henderson ▪ 702 435 2608 ▪ Open 10am–10pm daily ▪ www.ethelm.com

Take a free tour to view the glass-enclosed, spotless, white kitchens where the diligent candy-makers concoct their sweet creations. Find out what the large stainless steel machines do, and admire the finished confections wrapped in their foil of emerald, ruby, sapphire, and other jewel colors. Every participant receives a free chocolate at the end of the tour. Outside the factory is a lovely cactus garden, with plants clearly identified.

Las Vegas Motor Speedway

MAP E1 ▪ 7000 Las Vegas Blvd N. ▪ 702 644 4444 ▪ www.lvms.com

Completed in 1996, the 142,000-seat Las Vegas Motor Speedway was the first super-speedway to be built in the southwest USA in more than two decades. The 1,600-acre (647-ha) facility has 14 different race tracks, food courts, three levels of open-air grandstand viewing, VIP party rooms, and 102 luxury skybox suites. Important races staged here include NASCAR and National Hot Rod Association (NHRA) events. Visitors can take a lesson in race car driving

---

CASINOS BEYOND THE NEON

Although for the past few decades Las Vegas has been a sprawling city with shopping centers and clusters of businesses in the various neighborhoods, almost all of the hotel/casinos were concentrated in two areas – Downtown and along the Strip. In the 1980s, when the city's population began growing, a number of neighborhood hotel/casinos were built. Visitors who venture beyond the neon for gaming may be surprised to find very friendly and equally upscale casinos amid lovely surroundings (see p100).

---

from instructors at the Richard Petty Driving Experience. Concerts are sometimes held here as well, as is the annual Electric Daisy Carnival.

Henderson Farmers Market

200 S. Green Valley Pkwy, Henderson ▪ 702 579 9661 ▪ Open spring–early Fall: 9am–2pm Fri

Henderson's market had its beginnings in 1999 and gets bigger each season. Farmers drive from the California valleys to sell their produce year-round; in the summer season, they're joined by Nevada growers. Artisans sell everything from hand-painted china and rag dolls to house plants and chess sets.

NASCAR race at Las Vegas Motor Speedway

8 Rio Zipline

MAP P1 ■ Rio All-Suite Hotel & Casino, 3700 W. Flamingo Rd ■ 702 388 0477 ■ Open 11am–11pm daily ■ Adm ■ www.caesars.com/rio-las-vegas

The Rio's latest attraction consists of an absolutely terrifying thrill ride, on which riders race along a slender cable strung 500 ft (150 m) off the ground, with stunning city views. Mercifully, it's more like a ski lift than a traditional zip line, with each capsule holding two passengers at a time.

Rio's hair-raising Voodoo Zipline

9 Sunset Park

MAP D5 ■ 2601 E. Sunset Rd

One of the city's most popular parks, Sunset offers basketball and tennis courts, and jogging tracks; a place to fly kites and sail boats; and some of the best picnic spots in town. It also has a well-kept dog park, popular with local dog walkers.

10 Marjorie Barrick Museum

MAP Q4 ■ UNLV campus ■ 702 895 3381 ■ Open 9am–5pm Mon–Wed & Fri (to 8pm Thu), noon–5pm Sat ■ www.univ.edu/barrickmuseum

This small museum's collection focuses on modern art alongside Native American artifacts. It also contains exhibits exploring the area's anthropology, natural history and archaeology.

TWO EXCURSIONS BEYOND THE NEON

MORNING EXCURSION

Begin with an early-morning stroll around the **UNLV Campus**, stopping for a quick visit to the **Marjorie Barrick Museum**.

Drive to **Town Square Las Vegas** (see p73) where, if children are in your party, the play equipment will be the main attraction. Don't miss the shops while you're there. Then it's on to the **Ethel M Chocolate Factory** for the free tour and a walk around the cactus garden. Buy some chocolate for a local souvenir.

Before lunch, head to **Broadacres Marketplace** (open weekends only) for eclectic shopping and people watching, then stop by **Chinatown Plaza** for a bite to eat from one of the many Asian restaurants (see p97).

AFTERNOON EXCURSION

Begin the afternoon excursion at the **Nevada State Museum and Historical Society** (see p38) to learn more about the Silver State. Motor-racing fans should then make their next stop the **Las Vegas Motor Speedway**.

Those who want to try their hand at driving heavy equipment should stop by **Dig This** (see p97) for an exhilarating and unique experience. If you still have any energy left, **Sunset Park** is a great place to take a run or some time to relax if you prefer. Other outdoor areas offer opportunities for disc golf, hiking, and cycling. In the evening, visit a "locals casino" away from the Strip for a different dining and gaming experience (see p100).

See map on pp96–7

Casinos

Green Valley Ranch Resort

1 Green Valley Ranch Resort
2300 Paseo Verde Parkway, Henderson ■ 702 617 7777

Inspired by the great casinos of Europe, upscale Green Valley Ranch has over 2,000 slot and video poker machines and 55 table games.

2 Rampart Casino
MAP A3 ■ 221 N. Rampart Blvd ■ 702 867 5900

An intimate gaming atmosphere with a relaxing, upscale casino floor away from the crowds of the Strip.

3 Santa Fe Station
MAP A1 ■ 4949 N. Rancho Dr ■ 702 658 4900

Mid-size gambling floor (2,900 slots) and many entertainment options, the Santa Fe is patronized primarily by locals and is one of the more popular casinos beyond the neon.

4 Rio All-Suite Hotel & Casino
MAP P1 ■ 3700 W. Flamingo Rd ■ 866 746 7671

Home of the World Series of Poker, the Rio has more video machines than most, and relies on local trade for repeat business.

5 Boulder Station Hotel & Casino
MAP E4 ■ 4111 Boulder Hwy ■ 702 432 7777

Part of the Station's hotel-casinos chain, this one sports a railroad theme

and Victorian architecture. Head here for bingo, table games, and more than 1,600 video gaming machines.

6 Palace Station
MAP M1–2 ■ 2411 W Sahara Ave ■ 702 367 2411 ■ www.palace station.com

Situated a few miles west of the Strip, this plush casino offers bingo, keno, table games, video poker, and slots.

7 Sunset Station
MAP F6 ■ 1301 W. Sunset Rd, Henderson ■ 702 547 7777

Mediterranean-themed casino with wrought-iron balconies. Natural light makes it more pleasant than most.

8 Sam's Town
MAP E4 ■ 5111 Boulder Hwy, Las Vegas ■ 702 456 7777

One of the largest non-Strip casinos with thousands of slots, video poker, and keno machines.

9 The Orleans
MAP B4 ■ 4500 W. Tropicana Ave ■ 702 365 7111

There's a feeling of Mardi Gras in this casino, which is patterned after New Orleans' Vieux Carré.

10 Arizona Charlie's
MAP B3 ■ 740 S. Decatur Blvd ■ 702 258 5200

Dude-ranch theme touches include deer antler chandeliers. Pai Gow Poker and Royal Match 21 are included in the games.

Shopping

1 Chinatown Plaza
A shopping center (see p97) that serves the needs of the city's sizeable Asian community as well as visitors from around the world. At festival times (see p76), counters are piled high with moon cakes and treats linked to special days.

2 Las Vegas Premium Outlets
MAP C6 ■ 7400 Las Vegas Blvd S. ■ Open 11am–8pm Mon–Wed, 10am–9pm Thu–Sat (to 8pm Sun)
A truly fabulous place for shoppers who may have "champagne" tastes but "house-wine" wallets.

3 Antique Mall of America
9151 Las Vegas Blvd S. ■ Open 10am–6pm Mon–Sat
More than 100 booths selling an eclectic mix of antiques, collectibles, jewelry, art, furniture, and much more.

4 Bonanza Gift Shop
MAP M3 ■ 2440 Las Vegas Blvd S. ■ Open 8am–midnight daily
The store claims to be the largest gift shop in the world, with souvenirs ranging from T-shirts to the iconic green dealer's visors.

5 Cost Plus World Market
MAP A2 ■ 2151 N. Rainbow Blvd ■ Open 10am–8pm Mon–Fri (to 9pm Fri, 7pm Sun)
Large American retail chain with handsome tableware, furniture, foodstuffs, and art objects from all corners of the world at discount prices.

6 Fantastic Indoor Swap Meet
MAP B3 ■ 1717 S. Decatur Blvd ■ Open 10am–6pm Fri–Sun
The swap meet is the American equivalent of the European flea market: vintage kitchen appliances, tire chains, home-baked bread, mismatched chairs, etc.

7 Bass Pro Shops
MAP C6 ■ 8200 Dean Martin Dr ■ Open 9am–9pm Mon–Sat (to 7pm Sun)
Located at the Silverton Casino, this chain is known for its wide array of hunting, fishing, and outdoor gear.

8 Total Wine & More
730 Rampart Blvd ■ Open 8am–10pm daily
A massive store featuring 8,000 wines, 3,000 spirits, and 2,500 beers. The staff are very knowledgeable.

9 18b Arts District
MAP L3 ■ www.dtlvarts.com
This cultural district is home to many art galleries, studios, antique shops, and specialty stores.

10 Tivoli Village
400 S Rampart Blvd ■ Open 10am–8pm Mon–Thu (to 9pm Fri & Sat), 11am–6pm Sun
This shopping plaza has a plethora of stores, offering everything from cigars to jewelery, as well as live entertainment and food.

The exterior of Bonanza Gift Shop

See map on pp96–7

Bars and Nightlife

① Gaudi Bar
MAP F6 ■ Sunset Station, 1301 W. Sunset Rd ■ 702 547 7777 ■ Open 24hr daily ■ www. sunsetstation.sclv.com

Las Vegas's most extraordinary casino bar. This cavernous space, studded with mosaics and tiles, was designed and named in honor of Spanish architect Antoni Gaudí.

Stained-glass ceiling at Gaudi Bar

② Double Down Saloon
MAP Q3 ■ 4640 Paradise Rd ■ 702 791 5775 ■ Open 24hr daily ■ www.doubledownsaloon.com

Tiny dive bar near the Virgin Hotels, with street art murals, pool tables, and live punk, ska, and psychobilly bands nightly.

③ Flex Cocktail Lounge
MAP B3 ■ 4371 W. Charleston Blvd ■ 702 385 3589 ■ Open 24hr daily ■ www.flexlasvegas.com

Free nightly entertainment every night of the week at this legendary LGBTQ+ bar, including famous late-night drag shows on Wednesday and Saturday. Daily specials too.

④ Crown & Anchor
MAP R5 ■ 1350 E. Tropicana Ave ■ 702 739 8676 ■ Open 24hr daily ■ www.crownandanchorlv.com

This English-style sports pub in the university district is the place for watching live soccer, showing games from around the world. Traditional pub food is served 24 hours a day.

⑤ The Garage
MAP Q3 ■ 51487 E. Flamingo Rd ■ 702 440 6333 ■ Open 24hr daily

Welcoming neighborhood gay bar with a mechanic theme that will appeal to car enthusiasts.

⑥ Herbs & Rye
MAP C3 ■ 3713 W. Sahara Ave ■ 702 982 8036 ■ Open 5pm–3am Mon–Sat ■ www.herbsandrye.com

Cocktail lounge and tapas bar that evokes the spirit of a Prohibition-era speakeasy, with classic cocktails.

⑦ Stoney's Rockin' Country
MAP C5 ■ 6611 Las Vegas Blvd S. ■ 702 435 2855 ■ Open 7pm–2am Thu–Sat ■ www.stoneysrockin country.com

The city's biggest and wildest country bar puts on regular line dancing and live music.

⑧ Mermaid Bar & Lounge
MAP C6 ■ Silverton Casino, 3333 Blue Diamond Rd ■ 702 263 7777 ■ Open 10am–1am daily ■ www.silvertoncasino.com

This casino lounge lives up to its name – its aquarium tank is not only filled with fish but features water ballets by real (almost!) mermaids.

⑨ Piranha
MAP Q3 ■ 4633 Paradise Rd ■ 702 791 0100 ■ Open 10pm–5am Sun–Thu (to 6am Fri–Sat) ■ www. piranhavegas.com

Las Vegas's most spectacular gay nightclub, the epicenter of the so-called "Fruit Loop," offers an adjoining ultra lounge for VIPs.

⑩ The Railhead
MAP E4 ■ Boulder Station, 4111 Boulder Hwy ■ 702 432 7777 ■ Opening times vary ■ www. boulderstation.sclv.com

Lounge showroom in a lively neighborhood casino, with a varied program of rock, blues, and tribute bands, as well as dance nights.

Family Restaurants

1950s-style burger joint, Fatburger

1 Fatburger
MAP Q2 ▪ 3763 Las Vegas Blvd S. ▪ 702 736 4733 ▪ Open 10am–2am daily ▪ $

Big, handmade burgers and a classic 1950s atmosphere make Fatburger (see p68) a top Las Vegas hamburger destination.

2 BJ's Restaurant & Brewhouse
10840 W. Charleston Ave ▪ 702 853 2300 ▪ Open 11am–11pm daily ▪ $

Salads, sandwiches, pastas, and steaks, but the main draws are the pizzas and beers. Great lunch specials.

3 Buca di Beppo
MAP Q3 ▪ 412 E. Flamingo Rd ▪ 702 866 2867 ▪ Open 11am–10pm Mon–Thu (to 11pm Fri & Sat, to 9pm Sun) ▪ $$

There are family-style platters and hefty bottles of wine to be had at this authentic Italian dining experience.

4 Omelet House
MAP L2 ▪ 2160 W. Charleston Blvd ▪ 702 384 6868 ▪ Open 7am–3pm daily ▪ $

This low-key breakfast spot serves the under-10 crowd meals big enough to satisfy an adult.

5 Wienerschnitzel
MAP E4 ▪ 4680 E. Flamingo Rd ▪ 702 434 2955 ▪ Open 11am–11pm Sat–Thu (to midnight Fri) ▪ $

Drive-thru hotdog stand, with both the traditional dogs and variations.

6 Romano's Macaroni Grill
MAP C3 ▪ 2001 N Rainbow Blvd ▪ 702 648 6688 ▪ Open 11am–9pm Sun–Thu (to 10pm Fri & Sat) ▪ $

Bruschetta, fried mozzarella cheese, Italian panini sandwiches, and pasta.

7 Lotus of Siam
MAP Q4 ▪ 620 E. Flamingo Rd ▪ 702 735 3033 ▪ Open 11am–2:30pm Mon–Fri, 5:30–10pm daily ▪ $$

One of the finest Thai restaurants in Vegas, known for its excellent service.

8 Mimi's Café
6790 N. Durango Dr ▪ 702 645 3688 ▪ Open 7am–9pm daily ▪ $

Comfort food served in a warm atmosphere. Portions are large.

9 SkinnyFats
MAP E6 ▪ 140 S. Green Valley Pkwy ▪ 702 979 9797 ▪ Open 11am–11pm daily ▪ $

A modern, healthy restaurant offering many vegetarian and vegan options.

10 Original Pancake House
4170 S. Fort Apache Rd ▪ 702 433 5800 ▪ Open 7am–2pm Mon–Fri (to 3pm Sat & Sun) ▪ $

This place offers many varieties of divine pancakes in hearty portions.

Original Pancake House

See map on pp96–7

🔟 Lake Mead, Hoover Dam, and Laughlin

The Hoover Dam, most assuredly, changed the face of the American West. Not only did it enable the production of vast amounts of electrical energy and help to control floods, but it also provides water to cities and farms throughout the American Southwest and Mexico. The project's commercial byproducts in Nevada – Lake Mead and Boulder City, and the resort city of Laughlin – have infused billions of dollars into the state's economy and provided recreational opportunities for the hundreds of millions of visitors who come here every year.

Penstock towers, Hoover Dam

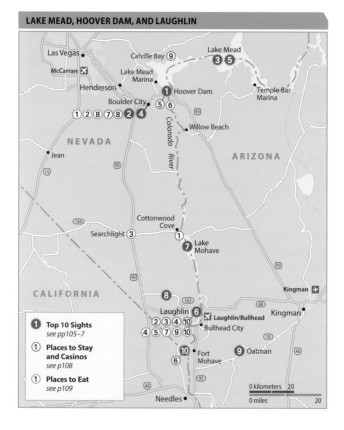

LAKE MEAD, HOOVER DAM, AND LAUGHLIN

① **Top 10 Sights**
see pp105–7

① **Places to Stay and Casinos**
see p108

① **Places to Eat**
see p109

Lake Mead National Recreation Area

1 Hoover Dam Tour

MAP T2 ■ Visitor Center, Hoover Dam: 702 494 2517 ■ Tour reservations: 866 730 9097 ■ www.usbr.gov/lc/hooverdam

Start at the three-story visitor center perched on the Nevada canyon wall. From here, Bureau of Reclamation guides offer tour options into the hydropower plant or the dam itself. Enjoy audio and film presentations, exhibits, and other media that tell the story of the Colorado River's settlement and the facts behind the technology involved in the distribution of water and production of hydroelectric power. From the top of the center, you can see the face of the dam, Lake Mead behind, and the Colorado River below *(see pp26–7)*.

2 Boulder City/ Hoover Dam Museum

MAP T2 ■ 1305 Arizona St, Boulder City; 702 294 1988 ■ Open 7am–7pm daily ■ Adm ■ www.bchdmuseum.org

Built in 1933, the Dutch Colonial-style Boulder Dam Hotel now houses the Boulder City/Hoover Dam Museum. Hollywood actors including Boris Karloff and Bette Davis stayed here during the hotel's glory days, and Crown Prince Olav and Princess Martha of Norway hosted a party here in 1939. The museum itself includes memorabilia and footage of the city from the 1930s. It also tells the story of the construction of the impressive Hoover Dam in the harsh Nevada Desert climate through personal histories and interactive displays *(see pp26–7)*.

3 Lake Mead National Recreation Area

MAP U2 ■ 601 Nevada Way, Boulder City ■ Alan Bible Visitor Center: 702 293 8990 ■ www.nps.gov/lake

After the completion of the Hoover Dam in 1935, the waters of the Colorado River filled the deep canyons that once towered above the river to create a huge reservoir. This lake, with its 550 miles (885 km) of shoreline, is the centerpiece of the 2,300-sq-mile (6,000-sq-km) Lake Mead National Recreation Area.

4 Boulder City Historic District

MAP T2 ■ Hoover Dam Museum; Hwy 93 at Lakeshore Rd; 702 294 1988

It's worth including Boulder City on a Hoover Dam trip to appreciate the scale of work involved – the city was built to house dam construction workers. The grandest buildings are the Bureau of Reclamation and the Bureau of Light headquarter buildings; the Municipal Building; and the Boulder Dam Hotel.

Boulder City Historic District

Entrance to Lake Mead Marina

5 Lake Mead Marinas and Beaches

MAP U2 ■ Alan Bible Visitor Center: 702 293 8990

Lake Mead's numerous marinas and beaches range from delightful tiny coves to long stretches of sand. Popular areas include Lake Mead RV Village, Echo Bay, Boulder Beach, Lake Mead Marina, and Temple Bar. These have recreational vehicle sites with full hookups, and supplies available from nearby stores. Boxcar and Icebox coves are favorites with houseboaters.

Petroglyphs near Laughlin

Callville Bay, Las Vegas Boat Harbor, and Lake Mead marinas are the closest ones to Hoover Dam, while Temple Bar marina serves the lake's southeasternmost reaches.

6 Laughlin's Casino Row

MAP T3 ■ 90 miles (145 km) S. of Las Vegas ■ www.visitlaughlin.com

The establishments lining Laughlin's South Casino Drive may not be as dazzling as those along the Las Vegas Strip, but they offer extremely good value. Getting around is easier than in Las Vegas: a riverwalk connects most of the casinos, or you can take a bus or shuttle boat. Tours of the Colorado River are also available.

7 Lake Mohave

MAP U2 ■ Part of Lake Mead National Recreation Area ■ Adm for park ■ www.nps.gov/lake

The 67-mile- (108-km-) long lake extends from below Hoover Dam to Davis Dam, 2 miles (3.2 km) north of Laughlin, and is only 4 miles (6.4 km) across at its widest point. A National Park Service Visitor Center at Katherine Landing, just north of Laughlin, offers free guided walks by park rangers. Boat rentals and fishing tackle are available at Katherine Landing, Willow Beach Marina, and Cottonwood Cove. Record-size striped bass have been caught in Lake Mohave.

8 Petroglyphs near Laughlin

MAP T3 ■ Part of Lake Mead National Recreation Area ■ www.nps.gov/lake

Christmas Tree Pass and Grapevine Canyon, just west of Laughlin on Hwy 163, are the best places to see the fascinating petroglyphs incised into the cliffs of the canyons by the early

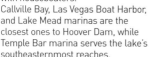

THE LAUGHLIN STORY

Don Laughlin opened his four-unit motel and bar with about a dozen slot machines on the banks of the Colorado River in the same week in 1966 as the opulent Caesars Palace opened in Las Vegas. Laughlin town (named by the postmaster in 1977) is now Nevada's third busiest gambling destination – outranked only by the major gaming centers of Las Vegas and Reno.

Patayan peoples. The line drawings and symbols may have served as the road maps of their day, directing hunters and fishermen. National Park Service personnel have located more than 150 Patayan camp sites between Davis Dam and Willow Beach, which is 10 miles (16 km) from the base of Hoover Dam.

9 Oatman, Arizona

MAP U3 ■ General information: 928 768 6222 ■ www.oatmangold road.org

A century ago, Oatman was a thriving gold mining center; today, visitors are taken back to the old days of the Wild West, with burros roaming the streets and staged gunfights in the middle of town. Honeymooners Clark Gable and Carole Lombard stayed here in 1939. A number of movies, including *How the West Was Won* have been shot in this town.

Donkeys on Main Street, Oatman

10 Avi Resort and Casino

MAP T3

In 1995, the Fort Mojave Indian tribe opened Nevada's first (and, in fact, the US's only) Native American-owned gaming business operated under state regulations. "Avi" means money or loose change. The resort *(see p108)* is in an area that the tribe intends to develop as a planned community.

TWO DAYS AT THE DAM AND LAUGHLIN

▶ **DAY ONE**

☕ Begin with early-morning coffee at **Railroad Pass Casino** on Hwy 93, an old-timer among gambling dens. Afterward, continue on Hwy 93 to the historic **Boulder City** and **Hoover Dam** *(see p105)* for the amazing tour.

Go back along Hwy 93 to the junction with Hwy 95 and turn south toward Laughlin. Stop at **Terrible's Roadhouse** *(see p109)* in Searchlight for lunch and the chance to visit a typical small-town Nevada casino.

For a more picturesque route, turn off Hwy 95 and head east on the dirt road through Christmas Tree Pass. Spend the remainder of the day in **Laughlin**, perhaps hunting for bargains at the 50-store Laughlin Outlet Center.

Stay overnight at **Harrah's** *(see p108)* or another hotel on the river, and be sure to take an evening stroll along its banks.

DAY TWO

Early next morning, golfers can tee off at any of the five area championship **Golf Courses**, where you can golf in two states (Nevada, and Arizona).

Later, head for **Oatman**, an old-time western town about a half-hour's drive southeast from Bullhead City. In the afternoon, drive back north to **Lake Mohave**. Be sure to make time to see the mysterious prehistoric petro-glyphs at **Grapevine Canyon**, off Hwy 163, before returning to your hotel in Laughlin.

See map on p104

Places to Stay and Casinos

1 Cottonwood Cove Resort & Marina

MAP U3 ▪ 10000 Cottonwood Cove Rd, Searchlight ▪ 702 297 1464 ▪ www.cottonwoodcoveresort.com ▪ $$$

Houseboats with a variety of sizes and facilities can be rented here. All you have to bring on deck is food, bedding, toiletries, and clothing.

2 Golden Nugget, Laughlin

MAP T3 ▪ 2300 S. Casino Dr ▪ 702 298 7111 ▪ www.golden nugget.com/laughlin ▪ $$

A tropical atrium with waterfalls, palm trees, and 300 species of tropical plants sets this hotel apart. The casino too is quite popular.

3 Don Laughlin's Riverside Resort, Laughlin

MAP T3 ▪ 1650 S. Casino Dr ▪ 702 298 2535 ▪ www.riverside resort.com ▪ $

This total destination resort has two classic auto showrooms and a display of antique slot machines. There's also an RV park with full amenities.

4 Aquarius Casino Resort, Laughlin

MAP T3 ▪ 1900 S. Casino Dr ▪ 702 298 5111 ▪ www.aquarius casinoresort.com ▪ $

The hotel features a large pool deck overlooking the river and Arizona hills, a fitness center, a wedding chapel, and Laughlin's largest tour boat, the *Celebration*.

5 Hoover Dam Lodge Hotel & Casino

MAP T2 ▪ 18000 Hwy 93, Boulder City ▪ 702 293 5000 ▪ www.hooverdam lodge.com ▪ $$

Located minutes from the Hoover Dam, this pet-friendly hotel offers casino gaming.

6 Avi Resort and Casino, near Laughlin

MAP T3 ▪ 10,000 Aha Macav Parkway ▪ 702 298 2535 ▪ $

This riverside resort *(see p107)* has a video arcade, a swimming pool, live entertainment, and 29 spa suites.

7 Quality Inn, Boulder City

MAP T2 ▪ 110 Ville Dr ▪ 702 293 6444 ▪ www.choicehotels. com ▪ $

Guests enjoy great views over Lake Mead at this 70-room motor hotel.

8 El Rancho Boulder Motel, Boulder City

MAP T2 ▪ 725 Nevada Hwy ▪ 702 293 1085 ▪ $

Spanish-style motel on the main street. Some rooms have kitchens.

9 Callville Bay, Lake Mead

MAP T2 ▪ On the north side of Boulder Basin ▪ 702 293 8990 ▪ www. callvillebay.com ▪ $

The campground offers showers, restrooms, a restaurant, lounge, and fuel. Reservations are not accepted.

10 Harrah's, Laughlin

MAP T3 ▪ 2900 S. Casino Dr ▪ 702 298 4600 ▪ www.caesars.com/ harrahs-laughlin ▪ $

Spanish-themed property with its own sand beach, a casino with a view and a pleasant ambience.

Harrah's, Laughlin

Places to Eat

1 Boulder Dam Brewing Company, Boulder City

MAP T2 ■ 453 Nevada Hwy ■ 702 243 2739 ■ www.boulderdambrewing. com ■ $

At this family restaurant, the walls display artifacts from the dam's construction. There is also a beer garden.

Boulder Dam Brewing Company

2 Toto's Mexican Restaurant, Boulder City

MAP T2 ■ 806 Buchanan Blvd ■ 702 293 1744 ■ www.totosmexican restaurantbc.com ■ $

Standard Mexican cuisine is done with flair at this popular chain.

3 Terrible's Roadhouse

MAP T2 ■ 100 Hwy 95 ■ 702 297 1201 ■ $

The signature dish here is a jumbo corn muffin with sausage, scrambled eggs, and gravy.

4 The Blues Brothers Tap House, Laughlin

MAP T3 ■ Tropicana Laughlin Hotel and Casino, 2121 S. Casino Dr ■ 888 888 8695 ■ Closed Mon–Wed, Thu–Sun L ■ $$

Gourmet flatbreads, burgers, and pizzas are staples at this microbrewery, which offers 16 beers on tap.

5 Bighorn Café, Laughlin

MAP T3 ■ Laughlin River Lodge, 2700 S. Casino Dr ■ 702 298 2242 ■ $

Delicious American cuisine is served under open-beam ceilings and in front of a roaring fire.

PRICE CATEGORIES

For a three-course meal for one with a half bottle of wine (or equivalent meal), including taxes, and extra charges.

$ under $30 $$ $30–$60 $$$ over $60

6 Bighorn Cafe

MAP T2 ■ 18000 Hwy 93, Boulder City ■ 702 293 5000 ■ www. hooverdamlodge.com ■ $

A full breakfast, lunch, and dinner menu is offered daily at this casual American restaurant.

7 Saltgrass Steak House, Laughlin

MAP T3 ■ 2300 S. Casino Dr ■ 702 298 7153 ■ www.goldennugget.com/ laughlin ■ $$

Frequented by a host of local families, Saltgrass offers affordably-priced cowboy-themed dishes.

8 Milo's Cellar, Boulder City

MAP T2 ■ 538 Nevada Hwy ■ 702 293 9540 ■ www.milosbouldercity. com ■ $

This sidewalk café, wine bar, and liquor store serves a variety of gourmet sandwiches, antipasti, and cheese platters, as well as hundreds of wines and over 40 types of beer.

9 Bubba Gump Shrimp Company, Laughlin

MAP T3 ■ Golden Nugget, 2300 S. Casino Dr ■ 702 298 7143 ■ www. bubbagump.com ■ $

At this seafood restaurant you can either sit indoors or outside under a covered patio.

10 The Prime Rib Room, Laughlin

MAP T3 ■ Riverside Casino, 1650 S. Casino Dr ■ 702 298 2535 ■ www. riversideresort.com ■ $$

The specialty at this restaurant is prime rib, carved at your table. However, there are other entrées, including chicken and fish.

See map on p104

🔟 Parks and Preserves

Less than an hour from the human-made extravaganzas and simulations of the Strip are natural wonders so dramatic and thrilling that humans could not begin to replicate them. Many of these wonders are geological phenomena formed millions of years ago. The closest is the magnificent desert region of Red Rock Canyon. Also nearby are Zion National Park, with its fantastic rock formations, and Death Valley – the hottest place in the world – whose floor lies 282 ft (86 m) below sea level, making it the lowest elevation in the western hemisphere. Most famous is undoubtedly the Grand Canyon, whose size and appearance are breathtaking. Each region has its distinct flora and fauna, with a number of species that are found nowhere else on Earth.

Desert View Watchtower

PARKS AND PRESERVES

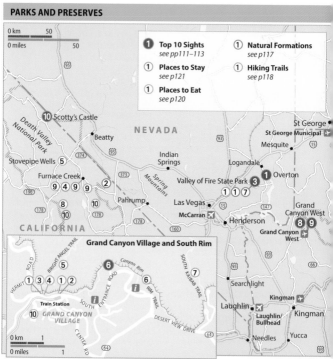

①	Top 10 Sights *see pp111–113*	①	Natural Formations *see p117*
①	Places to Stay *see p121*	①	Hiking Trails *see p118*
①	Places to Eat *see p120*		

Death Valley National Park
🔟 Scotty's Castle
Beatty
NEVADA
St George
St George Municipal ✈
Mesquite
Stovepipe Wells ⑤
Indian Springs
Logandale
Furnace Creek
⑨ ④ ⑨ ⑨   ②
Spring Mountains
Valley of Fire State Park ③   ① Overton
① ① ⑦
⑧
🔟   Pahrump
Las Vegas ✈
CALIFORNIA
McCarran ✈
Henderson
Grand Canyon West
⑧ ⑨
Grand Canyon West ✈

Grand Canyon Village and South Rim

HERMIT ROAD   BRIGHT ANGEL TRAIL
⑤   ⑥   Canyon Rim
① ③ ④ ① ②   ⑥   ⑦
SOUTH KAIBAB TRAIL
RIM TRAIL
Train Station
🔟   GRAND CANYON VILLAGE
SOUTH ENTRANCE ROAD   DESERT VIEW DRIVE   ⑭
CENTER RD   ⑭

Searchlight
Kingman ✈
Laughlin ✈
Laughlin/Bullhead   Kingman
Needles   Yucca

1 Lost City Museum, Overton

MAP U2 ■ 721 S. Moapa Valley Blvd, Overton ■ 702 397 2193 ■ Open 8:30am–4:30pm Wed–Sun ■ Adm ■ www.lostcitymuseum.org

Artifacts salvaged from Pueblo Grande de Nevada – now known as Nevada's "Lost City" – before it was inundated by Lake Mead are displayed at this pueblo-style museum opened in 1935. Exhibits include a village reconstruction, hunting weapons, and pottery.

2 Kolob Canyons, Zion National Park

MAP U1 ■ Kolob Canyons Visitor Center, east of exit 40 off 1-15 north, Utah ■ 435 772 3256 ■ www.nps. gov/zion

The Kolob Canyons section offers viewpoints of steep canyons and a 5-mile (8-km) scenic drive. It also

Kolob Canyons, Zion National Park

offers the closest access to Kolob Arch, which is one of the largest free-standing arches in the world.

3 Petroglyph Canyon, Valley of Fire

MAP U2 ■ 702 397 2088 ■ Adm for park ■ www.parks.nv.gov

Petroglyph Canyon is the Valley of Fire's most popular attraction, carrying as it does the park's largest concentration of petroglyphs – symbols and drawings incised on the rock faces by ancient Anasazi people from the Lost City. The purpose of the petroglyphs is unclear: some may have been no more than the road signs of their day, while others might have had a religious or mystical significance. The trail goes to Mouse's Tank.

4 Zion Canyon

MAP V1 ■ Zion Canyon Visitor Center; Hwy 9, nr Springdale; 435 772 3256 ■ Adm ■ www.nps. gov/zion

A shuttle system takes visitors along the scenic drive to the Temple of Sinawava (closed to private vehicles from March to November). Of special interest are the Court of the Patriarchs, the Streaked Wall, and the Virgin River. The Zion-Mt Carmel Highway is also a spectacular drive. If you can stay, head for Zion Lodge (see p121). Reserve a site early if you want to ensure a camping spot.

Stunning vistas of the Grand Canyon from Bright Angel Point, North Rim

⑤ Bright Angel Point, North Rim, Grand Canyon

MAP V2 ▪ North Rim Visitor Center, Bright Angel Peninsula ▪ Open mid-May–mid-Oct ▪ www.nps.gov/grca

The North Rim of the Grand Canyon may be more remote than the South Rim, but it is worth the effort. From the North Rim Visitor Center, walk the 0.25-mile (0.4-km) trail to Bright Angel Point for canyon views.

⑥ Yavapai Geology Museum, South Rim, Grand Canyon

MAP V2 ▪ 5 miles (8 km) N. of south entrance ▪ Open 8am–8pm daily (to 6pm in fall & winter)

For a visual introduction to Grand Canyon geology, you can scarcely beat the view from Yavapai Observation Station. Look down to the canyon floor for views of the Phantom Ranch

ANCIENT ROCKS

The Grand Canyon and Death Valley reveal more of the earth's geological history than anywhere else on the planet (some of its rocks are 1.7 billion years old). The mesas and cliffs of Zion National Park, too, were laid down and sculpted by the elements over millions of years. It is illegal to remove rocks or other artifacts from any national parks. Doing so, may cost you a heavy fine.

and the Colorado River. The river flows along the bottom of the canyon, a little less than 5,000 ft (1,500 m) below the rim. From this great height it doesn't look very threatening, but from the canyon floor it's a wildly impressive sight.

⑦ The Watchtower, Desert View, Grand Canyon

MAP V2 ▪ Hwy 64 at Desert View

A re-creation of an ancestral Puebloan tower, this landmark structure, designed by regional architect Mary Colter in 1932, is the highest point on the South Rim. The upper floor of the stone-built tower is decorated with Hopi murals. A gift store and refreshments are available. Other Colter designs at Grand Canyon include Hopi House, Hermits Rest, the Lookout Studio, and the cabins at Phantom Ranch.

⑧ Grand Canyon West

MAP U2 ▪ 928 769 2636 ▪ Open daily ▪ Adm ▪ www.grand canyonwest.com

This remote desert area, on the Hualapai Indian Reservation at the western end of the Grand Canyon, is the easiest part of the canyon to reach by air from Las Vegas. The car journey is long but the roads are paved. Besides the Skywalk, it offers tremendous canyon viewpoints and Western-themed attractions.

9 Skywalk, Grand Canyon West

MAP U2 ▪ 928 769 2636 ▪ Open daily ▪ Adm ▪ www.grandcanyon west.com

This iconic, horseshoe-shaped walkway, juts out from a red-rock clifftop above a 4,000-ft (1,200-m) drop at Grand Canyon West, and is best visited on a "flightseeing" day-trip. The gimmick, of course, is its see-through glass floor; it's perfectly safe, but you will need nerves of steel to take your first step.

10 Scotty's Castle, Death Valley

MAP S1 ▪ Hwy 267, at N. end of Death Valley ▪ Times vary, check website ▪ Adm ▪ www.nps.gov

Less of a castle and more of a Mediterranean-style mansion, the main human-made visitor attraction at Death Valley was built in the 1920s by the Chicago insurance magnate Albert Johnson. But Wild West show cowboy and conman Walter Scott had a habit of bragging that the spread was his, and it came to be called Scotty's Castle after him. A nice twist to the tale is that, in his last years, Scott was befriended by Johnson and spent his final years living at the coveted castle. Tours of the interior are available year round: fine craftsmanship is evident in the intricate wood carvings, wrought iron, and ornate tiling. Following a major flood in 2015, the castle has been undergoing extensive restorations.

Scotty's Castle, Death Valley

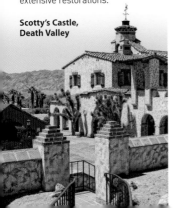

THREE TRIPS FROM VEGAS

It is not possible to do all trips in one day. Return to Las Vegas in between each place, making three separate excursions.

THE ROAD TO ZION

For a memorable overnight trip, drive east on Highway 15 to the turning for the **Valley of Fire**. Spend an hour or two on the park's scenic drive, hiking through **Petroglyph Canyon** *(see p111)* to **Mouse's Tank** *(see p118)* and visiting the **Lost City Museum** *(see p111)*. Then, back on Highway 15, proceed to **Mesquite** for lunch, making sure you are within reach of one of **Zion Canyon's** many viewpoints by sunset: you will be mesmerized. Spend the night camping in the park or at accommodation in **Springdale**.

GRAND CANYON

Take Highway 93 to **Kingman**, then Highways 40 and 64 to the national park. It is possible to view much of the canyon's natural grandeur by driving along the rim routes, but the total canyon experience involves hiking or riding to the valley floor, spending the night, and perhaps river-rafting. For insights into Native American culture, visit one of the reservations along the rim.

DEATH VALLEY

There are three major routes from **Las Vegas** to **Death Valley**. To choose the route most appropriate for your trip, visit www.nps.gov/deva for detailed information and planning tips. Bar food and spectacular scenery are available from Stovepipe Wells *(see p120)*.

See map on pp110–11

Local Flora and Fauna

1 Pine Forests
Dense forests of scrubby piñon pine, stunted by poor, dry soil, grow 6,500 ft (2,000 m) above sea level in the Grand Canyon (the canyon's highest elevation is 9,000 ft, or 2,750 m). About every seven years they produce bumper crops of edible nuts.

2 Wildflowers
Grand Canyon wildflowers include asters, sunflowers, globe mallows, and Indian paintbrushes. At Zion, look out for columbines, penstemons, Indian paintbrushes, and many varieties of sunflowers. Death Valley has fewer species, but Panamint daisies grow in profusion.

Indian paintbrushes

3 Sagebrush
The Nevada state flower is found up to 10,000 ft (3,000 m) above sea level and can grow as tall as 7 ft (2 m). These dense clusters of tiny yellow or cream flowers bloom in late summer.

4 Birds of Prey
Red-tailed hawks are the most common predatory birds in all three of the parks, but at the Grand Canyon look out for the king of the skies, the California condor.

5 Tortoises
Two species of desert tortoise, the Mojave and the Sonoran, are found in southern Utah, and in parts of Nevada and Arizona. These elusive creatures spend most of their lives underground.

6 Lizards
In Zion, eastern fence lizards are among 13 local species, while chuckwallas, short-horned, and collared lizards all inhabit the Grand Canyon and Death Valley. The banded lizard is most commonly spotted in Death Valley.

7 Bears
Black bears are occasionally seen on the higher plateaus at Zion, and more rarely on the North Rim of the Grand Canyon. The grizzlies have long since disappeared from the area, and no bears live in the Death Valley any longer.

8 Deer
The unmistakable stiff-legged jump and large ears of the mule deer distinguish it through your binoculars from its graceful relative, the white-tailed deer.

9 Snakes
Most species in the parks are harmless, but give rattlesnakes such as sidewinders a wide berth.

10 Mountain Lions
These shy creatures roam the Grand Canyon, Zion, and the mountains around Death Valley. They generally eat larger mammals such as mule deer and bighorn sheep.

One of Death Valley's mountain lions

Previous pages Red Rock Canyon

Natural Formations

① Atlatl Rock, Valley of Fire
MAP U2

The most famous petroglyph carved into this rock depicts an atlatl, a notched stick used to add speed and distance to a thrown spear.

② Funeral Mountains, Death Valley
MAP S1

A geological fault line was responsible for tilting these spectacular mountains on their sides.

③ Temple of Sinawava, Zion National Park
MAP V1

The temple is, in fact, an imposing and awe-inspiring mass of red rock. The religious name echoes many others in the park.

④ Great White Throne, Zion National Park
MAP V1

The sheer face of the Great White Throne, familiar to climbers worldwide, rises a staggering 2,200 ft (670 m) from the canyon floor, making it one of the tallest monoliths in the world.

⑤ Kolob Arch, Zion National Park
MAP V1

Kolob Arch is too inaccessible to permit accurate measurements of its bulk, but it is thought to be as much as 230 ft (70 m) high and 287 ft (87.5 m) wide.

⑥ Marble Canyon, Grand Canyon
MAP V2

The towering limestone walls of this canyon gave the upper section of the Grand Canyon its name.

Elephant Rock in the Valley of Fire State Park

⑦ Elephant Rock, Valley of Fire
MAP U2

Accessible via a short trail from the eastern entrance, this strange sandstone formation resembles the head of an elephant – albeit with an oversize trunk.

⑧ Inner Gorge, Grand Canyon
MAP V2

Sheer granite cliffs drop 1,000 ft (300 m) to the canyon floor to form this vertiginous gorge. Two nerve-testing suspension bridges make the crossing near Phantom Ranch.

⑨ San Francisco Mountains, Grand Canyon
MAP V2

Named the "Kingdom of St. Francis" by explorer Marcos de Niza, the range rises to an impressive height of 12,655 ft (3,857 m), the highest point in the state of Arizona.

⑩ Panamint Mountains, Death Valley
MAP S2

The Panamint Mountains are one of five mountain ranges in Death Valley. Head for Aguereberry Point to take in amazing views of the Funeral Mountains and the Sierra Nevada beyond.

See map on pp110–11

Hiking Trails

(1) Mouse's Tank, Valley of Fire

"Mouse" was the name of an American Indian outlaw. The moderately easy trail to Mouse's Tank (a series of natural catchments) passes the best petroglyphs in the park.

(2) Canyon Overlook Trail, Zion National Park

This moderate, short day-hike to the overlook provides great views of lower Zion Canyon.

(3) Observation Point Trail, Zion

The 8-mile (12.9-km) round-trip hike is moderately difficult to Hidden Canyon, then strenuous to Observation Point. There is a 2,148-ft (655-m) elevation gain.

(4) Riverside Walk, Zion

This paved walk at the base of a gorge is especially delightful in early November when the fall foliage is at its most beautiful.

(5) Bright Angel Trail, Grand Canyon

This popular 9.2-mile (14.8-km) trail drops 4,400 ft (1,342 m) to the Colorado River. You'll need two days – and a backcountry permit – to get to the river and back, so most visitors use the trail for shorter one-day hikes instead.

(6) Rim Trail, Grand Canyon

Extending from the Village area, the partially paved trail can be accessed at many points along Hermit Road and its terminus at the South Kaibab trailhead. There is little elevation change and great views.

(7) South Kaibab Trail, Grand Canyon

Access to the trailhead is by shuttle bus. The steep trail descends 4,500 ft (1,372 m), with no water along the down-and-back 14-mile (22.5-km) route.

(8) Wildrose Canyon to Wildrose Peak, Death Valley

A 4-mile (6-km) climb through woodland to the crest of the Panamint Mountains. Superb views.

(9) Golden Canyon to Zabriskie Point, Death Valley

A low-elevation, 6-mile (9.6-km) round-trip hike, traversing an area of fully exposed rock strata that represents millions of years.

(10) Coffin Peak Trail, Death Valley

This easy trail starts at Dante's View, following a canyon into the Black Mountains. Vegetation is dominated by spiny desert shrubs.

A view along the Bright Angel Trail, Grand Canyon

Commercial Tours

① GC Flight
702 629 7776 ▪ www.gc
flight.com
This company runs helicopter and
airplane flights, as well as motor-
coach tours, from Las Vegas to
the Grand Canyon and Hoover
Dam. Flights can also be taken
over the Strip.

② Maverick Helicopters
702 261 0007 ▪ www.
maverickhelicopter.com
The Wind Dancer Air and Landing
Tour includes landing on the floor
of the Grand Canyon, a champagne
picnic, and views of Lake Mead,
Hoover Dam, and an extinct volcano.

③ Awesome Adventures
866 548 4482 ▪ www.awesome
adventures.com
Several options for areas to tour
include the desert, Lake Mead,
and the Valley of Fire. Some tours
include lunch and hotel pick-up.

④ Grand Canyon Railway
800 843 8724 ▪ www.the
train.com
Grand Canyon Railway offers diesel-
powered and steam-train rides
between Williams and the South Rim.

**⑤ Zion Rock and
Mountain Guides**
435 772 3303 ▪ www.zionrock
guides.com
These expert guides and outfitters
are specialists in kitting out hikers
for the canyoneering day-hike
through Zion Narrows, in addition
to offering daily hiker shuttles and
climbing excursions.

**⑥ Zion Canyon
Field Institute**
435 772 3264 ▪ www.zionpark.org
This institute runs inexpensive
talks, walks, and expeditions in
Zion National Park, covering a broad
range of topics, such as history,
wildlife, photography, and geology.

Pink Adventure Tour in the desert

⑦ Pink Adventure Tours
800 873 3662 ▪ www.pink
adventuretours.com
Known for its knowledgeable guides,
Pink Adventure offers several half-
and full-day tours in the area. Tours
are conducted in 10-person vehicles,
so groups are kept to a manageable
size. It is also one of the few tour
companies with off-road permits.

⑧ Canyon Explorations
800 654 0723 ▪ www.canyon
explorations.com
One of several companies providing
hiking, interpretive trips, and white-
water rafting in the Grand Canyon.

**⑨ ATV & Jeep Adventure
Tours**
888 656 2887 ▪ www.atv
adventures.com
Year-round guided trips in four-
wheel all-terrain vehicles and Jeeps.
Three- to six-hour outings are
available. The company is based in
Hurricane, near St. George, Utah.

⑩ Adventure Photo Tours
702 889 8687 ▪ www.
adventurephototours.com
Full- and half-day tours hit highlights
so visitors have the chance to capture
ghost towns, wild horses, petroglyphs,
old mines, sandstone formations,
and wildflowers on camera.

See map on pp110–11

Places to Eat

El Tovar Dining Room

1 El Tovar Dining Room, Grand Canyon
MAP V2 ■ El Tovar Hotel, South Rim ■ 928 638 2631 ■ Open 7–10:30am, 11am–3pm & 4:30–9pm daily ■ $$
The pork porterhouse with prickly pear tequila glaze is the house specialty at this restaurant. It also serves fresh seafood that is flown in daily.

2 Coronado Room, Grand Canyon
MAP V2 ■ Best Western Squire Inn, Tusayan ■ 928 638 2681 ■ Open 5–10pm daily ■ $$
Prime rib and stuffed trout are favorites at this Spanish-style joint.

3 Fred Harvey Burger, Grand Canyon
MAP V2 ■ Bright Angel Lodge ■ 928 638 2631 ■ Open 11am–3pm daily ■ $
This family-friendly restaurant offers fresh diner-style fare.

4 Arizona Steakhouse, Grand Canyon
MAP V2 ■ Bright Angel Lodge ■ 928 638 2631 ■ $$
The all-American favorite spot that serves up big steaks, baked potatoes, and crisp salads.

5 Stovepipe Wells Village, Death Valley
MAP S2 ■ Stovepipe Wells ■ 760 786 7090 ■ Open 7–10am & 5:30–9pm daily ■ $
The Toll Road Restaurant offers eclectic fare all year long.

6 The Spotted Dog Café, Zion
MAP U1 ■ Springdale ■ 435 772 3244 ■ Open Mar–Nov: 5–9pm daily; Mar–Oct: 7–11am daily ■ $$
Among the house specialties are salads, pasta, red trout, chicken, Utah lamb, and Black Angus beef.

7 Picnic Areas, Zion Canyon and Springdale
MAP U1 ■ Sol Foods, 995 Zion Park Blvd ■ www.solfoods.com ■ $
Stock up on gourmet provisions at Sol Foods deli in Springdale for an alfresco meal in a nearby picnic area.

8 East Zion Thunderbird Lodge Restaurant, Mt. Carmel
MAP U1 ■ Mt. Carmel Jtn ■ 435 648 2203 ■ Open 7am–9pm Fri–Tue ■ $
American fare in a family dining room, where the pies, breads, and sweet rolls are all homemade.

9 The Inn at Death Valley Dining Room
MAP S1 ■ The Oasis at Death Valley ■ 760 786 3385 ■ Open May–Sep: 7–10am, 11:30am–2:30pm & 6–10pm daily; Oct–Apr: 5–9pm daily ■ $$$
Elegant dining room with lace tablecloths, firelight flickering on adobe walls, and views of the Panamint Mountains. Continental fare is served from a varied à la carte menu.

10 Maswik Lodge Cafeteria, Grand Canyon
MAP V2 ■ Maswik Lodge ■ 303 297 2757 ■ Open 6:30am–8pm daily ■ $
Wholesome food at reasonable prices. For a pre- or post-meal drink, the lodge includes a sports bar with a wide-screen TV.

Places to Stay

① Bright Angel Lodge, Grand Canyon

MAP V2 ■ South Rim ■ 928 638 2631 ■ www.grandcanyonlodges. com ■ $$

This lovely timber lodge consists of a rambling old building plus several private cabins, some right by the rim.

② El Tovar Hotel, Grand Canyon

MAP V2 ■ South Rim ■ 928 638 2631 ■ www.grandcanyonlodges.com ■ $$

Historic hotel built by pioneer resort builders, the Fred Harvey Company, in 1905. It is patterned after the great hunting lodges of Europe with a stone fireplace and mounted animals.

③ Grand Canyon Lodge

MAP V2 ■ North Rim ■ 877 386 4383 ■ www.grand canyonforever.com ■ $$

The only hotel accommodation on the North Rim of the canyon, this lodge comprises cabins and a few modern motel rooms. Advance reservations are essential.

④ The Inn at Death Valley

MAP S1 ■ Furnace Creek ■ 760 786 2345 ■ Open mid-Oct–mid-May ■ $$$

Elegant and expensive, the refurbished former Furnace Creek Inn offers glorious views of the Panamint Mountains.

Furnace Creek Inn, Death Valley

PRICE CATEGORIES

For a standard, double room per night (with breakfast if included), taxes, and extra charges.

$ under $100 $$ $100–200 $$$ over $200

⑤ Zion Lodge

MAP U1 ■ Zion National Park ■ 435 772 7700 ■ $$

The complex includes 40 cabins with gas log fireplaces, baths, and private porches, and 80 rooms, most with two queen-size beds.

⑥ Holiday Inn Express Springdale, Zion National Park

MAP U1 ■ 1215 Zion Park Blvd, Springdale ■ 435 772 3200 ■ $$

At the foot of The Watchman, the 120 rooms here are climate-controlled and some have kitchenettes.

⑦ Desert Pearl Inn, Zion

MAP U1 ■ 707 Zion Park Blvd, Springdale ■ 435 772 8888 ■ $$

Modern hotel by the Virgin River with great views, huge rooms, and a pool.

⑧ Camper Village, Grand Canyon

MAP V2 ■ Tusayan ■ 928 638 2887 ■ $

With 250 RV hook-ups and 100 tent sites, this is one of the larger, privately run, year-round campgrounds.

⑨ The Ranch at Death Valley

MAP S1 ■ Furnace Creek ■ 760 786 2361 ■ $$

The recently upgraded hotel offers two spring-fed pools, golf, tennis, and horseback riding.

⑩ Phantom Ranch, Grand Canyon

MAP V2 ■ Colorado River ■ 303 297 2757 ■ www.grandcanyon lodges.com ■ $

The only ranch at the bottom of the Grand Canyon. Only accessible to hikers and mule riders.

See map on pp110–11

Streetsmart

Fremont Street Experience

Getting Around

Arriving by Air

All international and domestic flights to and from Las Vegas use **McCarran International Airport**. Although the runways are close to the southern end of the Strip, it is 3 miles (5 km) by road from the terminals to the nearest part of the Strip, and 7 miles (11 km) to Downtown. Allow at least 10 minutes to travel between the airport and hotels on the Strip; in rush-hour traffic (weekdays 7–9am and 4–7pm) the trip can be very slow.

As the Las Vegas Monorail does not serve the airport, the easiest way to reach your accommodation is by taxi, which will cost anything from $16 to the southern end of the Strip to $30 for Downtown (rides with Uber or Lyft will cost less). Standard cabs charge a starting fee of $5 and rates depend on the driving time, so it can be expensive if you're in rush-hour traffic.

It is also possible to ride in a shared **Bell Trans Airport Shuttle** bus, which takes passengers on request to hotels. However, if your hotel is low on the list it can take an hour or more to reach it.

The Centennial Express (CX) public bus connects the airport with the Strip and Downtown every 30 minutes in peak hours; hourly off-peak. On the Strip it operates only at Tropicana Avenue and Las Vegas Boulevard. Rent a car if you plan to travel beyond the city.

There are no car rental agencies at the airport itself but you can pick up cars from the McCarran Rent-A-Car Center (see p127), 3 miles (5 km) southwest, which is easily reached using the free shuttle buses that stop outside both of the terminals.

Long-Distance Train Travel

Las Vegas does not have an Amtrak station. The Kingman Amtrak station in the neighboring state of Arizona is the closest train station. From there it's a 1.5-hour car journey to Las Vegas. Train timetables can be found on the **Amtrak** website.

Long-Distance Bus Travel

Long-distance buses, operated by **Greyhound** run to the city from Los Angeles (taking between 5 and 7 hours) and Salt Lake City (taking around 8 hours), both of which are served by Amtrak trains, and from Phoenix, which is not. Las Vegas's Greyhound station is Downtown, beside the Plaza hotel.

Public Transportation

The **Regional Transportation Commission (RTC)** is the main public transport authority in Las Vegas. Safety and hygiene measures, timetables, ticket information, transport maps, and more can be obtained from RTC kiosks or the RTC website.

Buses

The RTC runs a comprehensive network of buses throughout the city. Most visitors, however, use its two principal routes, the Deuce and the Strip & Downtown Express (DVX), both of which are wheelchair accessible. The Deuce runs 24 hours daily along the entire Strip, from Mandalay Bay to the Stratosphere, stopping outside every major casino, and also continues north into and around Downtown.

The DVX (which also runs 24 hours daily) starts at the South Strip Transfer Terminal (SSTT), 3 miles (5 km) south of Mandalay Bay, which is served by separate buses to and from the airport. It runs north along the Strip, stopping opposite Mandalay Bay, and outside the MGM Grand, Paris, and Wynn; it then heads, via the Convention Center and Fremont Street Downtown, to the Las Vegas Premium Outlets (North) shopping center. On its return journey south, back along the Strip, it stops outside the Fashion Show Mall, Bellagio, Excalibur, and Mandalay Bay. To board a bus, you have to buy a ticket from the machines located next to each stop. A 2-hour pass costs $6, a 24-hour pass $8, and a 3-day pass $20.

Many off-Strip casino hotels offer free shuttle

buses to and from the Strip, although some are reserved only for hotel guests.

Monorail

The **Las Vegas Monorail** runs parallel to the Strip on its eastern side, from the MGM Grand to the SLS hotel via the Convention Center (7am–midnight Mon, 7am–2am Tue–Thu, 7am–3am Fri–Sun). It does not serve the airport or Downtown. As the stations are a long way back from the Strip, it is only useful for longer journeys. A one-ride ticket costs $5, a one-day pass $13, and a three-day pass $29.

In addition, three free smaller-scale tram systems link some of the casinos on the west side of the Strip. One connects Excalibur with Luxor and Mandalay Bay; another runs from Bellagio to Park MGM, via Aria and the Crystals mall; and the last travels between TI and The Mirage.

Taxis

Taxis cannot be hailed on the street (safety laws prohibit them from stopping) but there are designated taxi stands at most resorts, shopping malls, and attractions. Hotel entrances on the Strip and Downtown are the best places to get cabs. The standard fare includes an initial fee of $3.50, plus $2.76 for each additional mile, and about 50 cents a minute when stopped at a red light or stalled in traffic. In heavy traffic, it can cost more than $20 to go from one end of the Strip to the other. You can also call

for a pickup. **Yellow-Checker-Star (YCS) Taxicabs**, **Lucky Cab** and **Nellis Cab** are just a few local taxicab firms.

Rideshare options Uber and Lyft are as popular as standard cabs. All of the casino hotels include rideshare service pickups and dropoffs in their designated cab areas.

Limousines

Perhaps the ultimate Las Vegas travel experience is the limousine. Hire a limo for a special occasion or for when you want to step out in style. Limos include stretch and superstretch versions that are fitted out with a cocktail bar, moon roof, and even a Jacuzzi.

Presidential Limo is a popular company. Hourly rates start at around $60 for a town car and go up to about $130 for a 12-passenger stretch limo with complimentary champagne. Rent a party bus seating 20 for around $190 an hour.

Trips and Tours

Pink Jeep Tours offers four-wheel-drive tours and **Gray Line** runs bus tours farther afield to the Hoover Dam and Grand Canyon National Park. Among the most popular types of excursions are aerial tours, ranging from 15-minute flights over the Strip to trips to the Grand Canyon. **Canyon Tours** runs flights in small planes or helicopters over both Las Vegas and the Grand Canyon. They also do rafting, and even jet ski tours. Most packages include pick-up and drop-off at your hotel.

Driving to Las Vegas

The main and busiest driving route to and from Las Vegas is the I-15 interstate, which connects the city with Salt Lake City in Utah, 420 miles (676 km) northeast, and Los Angeles in California, 270 miles (435 km) southwest. On Friday evenings in particular, the road is usually crammed with visitors heading up from LA for the weekend. It is best to stay on the interstate until you're as close as possible to your hotel; driving on the Strip is generally much slower.

Arriving from the east or Arizona, you're most likely to approach Las Vegas along the I-11 freeway, which crosses into Nevada near the Hoover Dam. This road runs straight to Downtown; turn off west to get to the Strip.

Driving in Las Vegas and Surrounding Areas

Although cruising along the Strip can be a real thrill, driving is not a quick or convenient way to get from casino to casino. A car is essential, on the other hand, if you plan to explore the outlying neighborhoods of Las Vegas, or to venture anywhere beyond the city. Nearly all of the Strip hotel and casinos charge for parking in high-rise garages at the back (with quick, easy access into the casinos), as well as more expensive valet parking. Downtown, parking is generally more restricted; most Fremont Street hotels require you to join their rewards program for free parking.

The panoramic wilderness of southern Utah, California, and Arizona surrounds the city and forms a landscape filled with awe-inspiring canyons and parks, such as The Grand Canyon and Zion National Park. Public transportation to these areas is limited so hiring a car is the best way to reach them. The area is served by a network of well-maintained roads, from multi-lane highways to scenic routes.

Rules of the Road

Highway speed limits vary from state to state, but in no instance are speeds in excess of 75 mph (120 km/h) permitted. Cars that pull trailers or campers are restricted to 55 mph (90 km/h). Always be aware of the posted speed limits because they vary from state to state, and can be altered because of ongoing construction or changing weather conditions. In Nevada the speed limit on freeways is 70–80 miles/113–130 km/h and in residential areas it's 20–30 miles/32–48 km/h.

The highway patrol in Nevada and other states are in charge of enforcing the highway laws and speeding violations are usually accompanied by a strict fine. Also note that drivers can be cited for driving too slowly on the interstates.

Law requires that the driver and passengers wear seat belts. It is illegal to pass a stationary school bus when students are boarding and departing or when the bus is flashing its red lights. The most serious offence, however, is driving under the influence of alcohol or other substances. The legal limit is 0.08 BAC (Blood Alcohol Concentration) and heavy penalties are exacted from those who violate these laws. Unless a sign says otherwise, you can turn right after stopping at a red light if there is no oncoming traffic, and the first vehicle to reach a four-way stop sign junction has the right of way. Note that hitchiking is illegal throughout Nevada.

Maps and more information on driving rules can be obtained from your car rental agency or from the **American Automobile Association (AAA)**.

For exploring any of the remote wilderness areas surrounding Las Vegas, it is important to check if a four-wheel-drive vehicle is required. Many of the backcountry areas can be accessed only by "fire roads," which are unpaved or dirt roads. Maintenance agencies, such as the US Forest Service at Mount Charleston and the Bureau of Land Management at Red Rock Canyon, can provide up-to-date maps and tips. Plan your route carefully in advance. If you are traveling between remote locations, let the park warden or caretaker know about your itinerary. Check the road conditions before you start by consulting the **NV Roads** website for alerts, and be aware of seasonal dangers such as flash floods, which can occur with little warning in the Southern Nevada desert. Do not drive off-road unless in a specially designated area.

Car Hire

Visitors from abroad must have an international driver's license. Although it is legal to rent a car to those over the age of 21, most rental companies charge extra to those under 25. It is essential to have a credit card to pay the rental deposit as few companies are willing to accept a cash deposit. Drivers must have their license with them and carry the car rental contract at all times.

There are no car rental chains at McCarran International Airport. Car rental companies operate from the **McCarran Rent-A-Car Center**, just off the Strip 3 miles (5 km) south of Mandalay Bay, and the same distance southwest of the airport, to which it's connected by frequent free shuttles. Renting a compact car here typically costs from around $50 per day, or $250 per week. Although you can rent a car at all the major hotels, you'll almost certainly pay much higher rates if you do. For an extra $20–30 you can purchase a collision damage waiver, which saves you from being charged for any visible defects on the car.

Most rental cars have automatic transmission. Child seats or cars for disabled drivers must be arranged in advance.

Cycling

Las Vegas is not a particularly bike-friendly city because of heavy traffic congestion and a general lack of cycling infrastructure. Though cycling along the main arteries is not advised, riding around Downtown, residential neighborhoods and in outlying scenic areas, such as Red Rock Canyon and Lake Mead, can be very enjoyable. Many streets in the residential areas of Las Vegas have designated bike lanes, but biking along the congested Strip is not recommended and many other areas of the city don't have cycle lanes. Be sure to wear a safety helmet when cycling and carry water, especially during the summer heat.

The **RTC Bike Share** scheme has about 200 classic and electric bikes at multiple rental pods in Downtown Las Vegas. A Dasher Pass costs $5 per day and includes an unlimited number of 30-minute rides; it's another $4 per 30 minutes after the first 30 minutes. **Las Vegas Cyclery** is a handy bike rental store and **Bike Blast Las Vegas** conducts guided tours in desert and mountain areas beyond the Strip and Downtown.

Walking

Walking is the best way to explore the Strip and the Downtown area. You may be surprised by quite how much you walk in Las Vegas; it can take upwards of ten minutes to walk from one casino to the next, while the entire Strip stretches for 4 miles (6 km). Casinos are well connected, sidewalks are wide, and the terrain is flat, but in summer the heat can be merciless so be sure to drink plenty of water. By walking you can explore most major sights and shopping areas without worrying about the traffic or spending time searching for a parking place. **Las Vegas Walking Tours** runs guided walks through Downtown historic Fremont Street.

Beyond the Strip itself and the small Downtown, distances are large, and most people drive or take public transportation.

Practical Information

Passports and Visas

For information on entry requirements, including visas, consult your nearest US embassy or check the **US Department of State** website. Canadian visitors require only a valid passport to enter the US. Citizens of Australia, New Zealand, the UK, and the EU do not need a visa but must apply in advance for an Electronic System for Travel Authorization (**ESTA**) visa waiver and have a valid passport. All other visitors will need a valid passport and visa waiver to enter.

Government Advice

Now more than ever, it is important to consult both your and the US government's advice before traveling. The **UK Foreign and Commonwealth Office**, the US Department of State, and the **Australian Department of Foreign Affairs and Trade** offer the latest information on security, health, and local regulations.

Customs Information

You can find information on the laws relating to goods and currency taken in or out of the US on the **US Customs and Border Protection Agency** website.

Insurance

We recommend that you take out a comprehensive insurance policy, covering theft, loss of belongings, medical care, cancellations, and delays, and read the small print carefully. There is no universal healthcare in the US for citizens or visitors and healthcare is very expensive so it is particularly important to take out comprehensive medical insurance. In most cases, people incurring medical expenses are required to pay before leaving the treatment center. Keep receipts to make a claim on your insurance later.

Health

The US has an excellent private healthcare system. In Las Vegas, both the **Sunrise Hospital** and the **University Medical Center** have 24-hour emergency rooms. Pharmacies are a very good source of advice, too. They can diagnose minor ailments and suggest appropriate treatment. The main pharmacy chains are **CVS** and **Walgreens**. Pharmacies on the Strip include the 24-hour CVS beside the Park MGM and Walgreens next to The Palazzo.

When out and about, beware of over-exposure to the sun. Use high-factor sun creams, especially when swimming, and drink plenty of fluids.

Beware of rattlesnakes and scorpions in the desert. Before you go, learn how to treat their bites (getting medical help as quickly as possible). Other dangerous desert animals and insects are mountain lions, bears, wild boar, killer bees, and centipedes. Wildlife may seem tame but will attack if it feels threatened.

Unless otherwise stated, tapwater is safe to drink in the US.

No inoculations are required to visit the US. For information regarding COVID-19 vaccination requirements, consult government advice.

Smoking, Drugs, and Alcohol

Smoking is prohibited in many indoor public spaces, including restaurants, malls, grocery stores, and non-gaming areas of casinos, but is permitted in bars that do not allow guests under the age of 21.

The legal minimum age for drinking alcohol is 21, and even those who look obviously older will need photo ID as proof of age in order to purchase alcohol.

Marijuana was legalized for recreational use in Nevada in 2016 but the law prohibits public consumption of marijuana in all public places. Anyone who violates this law could face a fine or a prison sentence. Possession of illegal drugs is prohibited everywhere and could result in a hefty prison sentence.

ID

It is not compulsory to carry ID at all times. If you are asked by police for your ID, a photocopy of your passport photo page (and visa if applicable) should suffice. You may be asked to present the original document within 12 or 24 hours.

Personal Security

Las Vegas is generally a safe place, and by exercising common sense, your visit should be trouble-free. Beware of pickpockets in crowds (especially on public transportation), keep cash and valuables well hidden, and be vigilant in multi-story parking garages.

If you have anything stolen, report the crime within 24 hours to the nearest police station and take ID with you. Get a copy of the crime report in order to claim on your insurance. Contact your embassy if you have your passport stolen, or in the event of a serious crime or accident.

For emergency police, fire, or ambulance, dial the emergencies number 911 free of charge from any phone.

With a reputation for being laid-back and progressive, the people of Nevada are, as a rule, accepting of everyone, regardless of their race, gender or sexuality. Same-sex marriage has been legal since 2014 *(see p133)* and the state recognizes the rights of those legally wanting to change their gender. Las Vegas has a thriving LGBTQ+ scene, with plenty of LGBTQ+ bars, clubs, and events on and off the Strip. **Gay Vegas** is a comprehensive source of information about LGBTQ+ events, restaurants, bars, hotels, and more.

Travelers with Specific Requirements

Las Vegas is one of the most accessible cities in the US for those with disabilities. The vast majority of sights and attractions, including casinos and venues hosting shows, are wheelchair-accessible. Many casinos offer braille bingo. Detailed information is provided on the "Travelers with Special Needs" page of the **Las Vegas Convention and Visitors Center Authority (LVCVA)** website.

Every taxi firm has lift-equipped vans. Both Bell Trans Airport Shuttle and RTC city buses *(see pp124 & 125)* are wheelchair-accessible.

All car-rental chains offer adapted vehicles, and the **Nevada Department of Motor Vehicles** will issue visitors free, short-term disabled parking permits. Mobility equip-ment can be rented from the **Ability Center**.

Time Zone

Las Vegas operates on Pacific Standard Time, which is three hours behind Eastern Standard Time, and eight hours behind Greenwich Mean Time. Clocks move one hour forward on the second Sunday in March, and one hour back on the first Sunday in November.

DIRECTORY

PASSPORTS AND VISAS

ESTA
🌐 esta.cbp.dhs.gov

US Department of State
🌐 state.gov

GOVERNMENT ADVICE

Australian Department of Foreign Affairs and Trade
🌐 smartraveller.gov.au

UK Foreign and Commonwealth Office
🌐 gov.uk/foreign-travel-advice

CUSTOMS INFORMATION

US Customs and Border Protection Agency
🌐 cbp.gov/travel

HEALTH

CVS
🌐 cvs.com

Sunrise Hospital
MAP N5 ▪ 3186 S. Maryland Pkwy
🌐 sunrisehospital.com

University Medical Center
MAP K2 ▪ 1800 W. Charleston Blvd
🌐 umcsn.com

Walgreens
🌐 walgreens.com

PERSONAL SECURITY

Gay Vegas
🌐 gayvegas.com

TRAVELERS WITH SPECIFIC REQUIREMENTS

Ability Center
🌐 abilitycenter.com

Las Vegas Convention and Visitors Center Authority (LVCVA)
🌐 lasvegas.com

Nevada Department of Motor Vehicles
🌐 dmvnv.com

Money

The official currency of the United States is the US dollar.

Major credit, debit, and pre-paid currency cards are widely accepted, as are device contactless payments. It is useful to have bills of various sizes to hand, however, for tipping. In restaurants it is normal to tip 18–25 per cent of the total bill. Allow for a tip of 15 per cent for taxi drivers and $1 per drink or 15 per cent per round for casino or bar staff. Hotel porters and housekeeping expect $1–$2 per bag or per day.

Banks are few and far between, and especially rare on the Strip, and while cashiers' offices in all the casinos will exchange foreign money, they charge punitive rates. Almost all ATMs in the city charge a fee for each cash withdrawal, typically $3.

Electrical Appliances

As throughout the US, the electrical current in Las Vegas is 110 volts and 60 hertz. Visitors from abroad will need a Type A or Type B adaptor plug to use the two-prong sockets, and may also need a voltage converter to operate their own appliances. Most charging leads for foreign phones and laptops incorporate voltage converters that will work in the US.

Cell Phones and Wi-Fi

All Las Vegas hotels offer in-room Wi-Fi. It is not exactly free – it's one of the main elements of the so-called "resort fees" charged by most hotels. The fee may only cover one device; a couple traveling with a smartphone and a laptop each may have to pay four times over. Many casino-hotels offer free Wi-Fi in their public areas. You can also get free Wi-Fi at the airport, in coffee bars, and in Apple stores. **WiFi Map** is a handy app that finds free Wi-Fi hotspots near you.

Cell phone service in Las Vegas is generally good. To avoid roaming charges buy a SIM from a US provider, such as **AT&T**.

Postal Services

USPS (US Postal Service) runs the postal system in the US. The Las Vegas Main Post Office is generally open 8am–9pm Monday to Friday and 8am–4pm on Saturday.

Weather

Las Vegas is a desert city, receiving an average of just 4 inches (10 cm) of rainfall per year. The summer is excruciatingly hot, with average daily highs in July and August of well over 100 °F (38 °C). Winter is less predictable; the nights can drop below freezing in December and January, but conditions may be balmy during the day. The best seasons to visit are spring and fall.

The weather can present a variety of dangers, especially in the canyons, where sudden summer storms can cause flash floods. Don't try to drive through flooded areas. If water begins to rise over the road, it is actually best to abandon your car and move to high ground. If you are going for a hike, always notify someone of your route and when you expect to return. Never venture into the desert alone, and don't go hiking without a map and a good compass. The dry heat of the summers is merciless, and hikers are advised to carry at least a gallon (4 liters) of drinking water per person for each day of walking.

Carry water for your car engine, too. It is also important for visitors to guard against the risk of forest fires, which can have devastating effects on the area.

Opening Hours

COVID-19 Increased rates of infection may result in temporary opening hours and/or closures. Always check ahead before visiting museums, attractions, and hospitality venues.

Shops and attractions on the Strip and Downtown open every day of the week at 9am or 10am and remain open well into the evening, especially on weekends.

Casinos are open all day, as are some restaurants and bars, and can be busy at both 3am and 3pm.

Visitor Information

Las Vegas's main tourist body, the LVCVA (see p129) runs a visitor center at 3150 Paradise Road and has an excellent website with details of accomm-odations, attractions, and shopping. Visitors can also check the **Downtown Vegas Alliance**, **Rate Vegas**, and **Vegas.com** websites for details on where to go and what to do in the city. **Travel Nevada** offers ideas for road trips and activities throughout the state.

There are a number of discount cards for tourists. **GoCity** offers passes with 55 per cent off many sights in Las Vegas. The **Las Vegas Bite Card** offers buy-one-get-one-free tickets for the most popular shows and half-price meals at certain restaurants.

Taxes and Refunds

Taxes will be added to hotel and restaurant charges, theater tickets, some grocery and store sales, and most other purchases. Always check if tax is included in the price displayed. Sales tax is around 8 per cent.

Accommodation

The Strip consists almost exclusively of massive casinos that are also hotels – so much so that more than half of the world's 40 largest hotels are concentrated along its stretch. In addition to an extensive gambling area, each holds a number of restaurants, bars, shops, nightclubs, and one or more theater-sized showrooms. Even if you're not interested in gambling, it makes sense to stay in one of the hotels that make Las Vegas what it is. Their thousands of guest rooms are located in high-rise towers that soar above the casino itself,

and thus well removed from the frenzy below. Typical rooms tend to resemble what you would find in an upscale hotel elsewhere – they are seldom themed like the casinos. Staying in such enormous hotels does of course have its downsides. You may well have to wait half an hour or more to check in when you first arrive, while in a property like The Venetian it can take twenty minutes to walk from your room to the Strip sidewalk.

There are strong arguments in favor of staying Downtown rather than on the Strip. Apart from the Golden Nugget (see p55), the Downtown options are much more manageable in scale, and generally somewhat cheaper. Downtown also conforms to a more old-fashioned neighborhood feel.

Countless ordinary chain hotels and motels line the streets within a mile or two of the Strip, while outlying casino-hotels are found around the rest of the city. It is really only practical to stay in those areas if you have a car. It can be unpleasant to walk even half a mile between your hotel and the Strip, along the traffic-choked streets in the desert heat.

Beware that every room in every hotel changes in price every night. A room that costs $70 on Monday or Tuesday can easily cost $220 that same Friday or Saturday. To save money, time your visit for week-days rather than week-ends. It may be worth changing to a cheaper hotel for the weekend; stay on the Strip during the

week and move Downtown for the weekend. Major concerts, conventions, and events will increase prices of hotel rooms.

Make bookings well in advance. You will find the cheapest rates on the websites of the casinos themselves. Comparison shopping is easy: there is a hotel booking facility on the LVCVA website (see p129).

Room rates quoted online won't include either the compulsory "resort fees" charged by the casinos for facilities such as in-room Wi-Fi, which typically cost an additional $17–45 per night, or room taxes, which add up to 13.35 per cent.

DIRECTORY

CELL PHONES AND WI-FI

AT&T
w att.com

WiFi Map
w wifimap.io

POSTAL SERVICES

USPS (US Postal Service)
w usps.com

VISITOR INFORMATION

Downtown Vegas Alliance
w downtown.vegas

GoCity
w gocity.com

Las Vegas Bite Card
w vegasbitecard.com

Rate Vegas
w ratevegas.com

Travel Nevada
w travelnevada.com

Vegas.com
w vegas.com

Getting Married in Las Vegas

Las Vegas Weddings

Getting married continues to rank among the major reasons to come to Las Vegas – the bureaucracy is minimal, the costs are (or at least can be) comparatively low, and, of course, it is a great place to have a party. While the spontaneous ceremony in the dead of night may be a staple of Hollywood movies, most Las Vegas weddings are far from kitsch or frivolous, and the wedding industry is a multimillion-dollar business here.

All the major casinos have their own chapels and wedding-planning services, while countless private chapels are dotted around the city, and especially along the stretch of Las Vegas Boulevard that runs south from Downtown to the Strip proper. Almost all of them are capable of hosting opulent weddings if you are happy to pay the appropriate price; be warned, though, that at the cheaper end of the market they can be somewhat dispiriting and soulless places. Las Vegas chapels celebrate around 100,000 weddings each year.

The two busiest periods are Valentine's Day and New Year's Eve, which besides being romantic dates offer the prosaic advantage for US couples of entitling them to submit a joint tax return for the preceding year. Couples planning their wedding around those times should obtain licenses well in advance, to avoid long lines at the **Clark County Marriage License Bureau**.

Laws and Licenses

The marriage-license requirements in Nevada have traditionally been less stringent than those in other US states. No blood tests are needed, and neither is it necessary, after the license has been issued, to wait a set period before getting married.

To obtain a license, both partners must appear at the County Clerk's office in the Clark County Marriage License Bureau, in Downtown Las Vegas. Both must be aged over 18 and carrying picture ID. Anyone aged between 16 and 18 must either have a consenting parent present, or be able to produce a notarized document from a parent giving his or her consent. Acceptable forms of ID are listed on the bureau's website. US citizens must also provide their Social Security numbers, but do not have to show the actual Social Security card. Applicants who have been married before must provide details of when and where their divorces were finalized, or if their previous partners died, but do not have to show copies of divorce decrees or death certificates.

The marriage license costs $102, payable in cash or by credit or debit card. The process is quicker if you have already completed the application form online, using the bureau's website, in which case you simply need to take your reference number to the office's "express window."

Wedding Ceremonies

Nevada law requires that couples be married by civil marriage commissioners, justices of the peace, or bona fide ministers. The fastest and least expensive way to get married is to walk from the Clark County Marriage License Bureau to the **Office of Civil Marriages**, where the commissioner will perform a civil ceremony for $75 plus a transaction fee, payable by credit or debit card. You can only do so, however, if you have made an appointment in advance, which is only possible via the Clark County website.

Be sure you go to the genuine Office of Civil Marriages; some wedding chapels deliberately give themselves very similar names to fool couples into paying for their ceremonies instead. In addition, touts wait outside hoping to lure couples away to nearby chapels.

Note that a witness is required at all marriages. It is much better to bring someone you know to act as a witness, rather than to ask a stranger hanging around outside the office.

Costs and Options

The cheapest ceremony at a Las Vegas wedding chapel is liable to cost around $200. Expect to pay around $75 for the use of the chapel itself – or, in the case of the drive-through facility at **A Little White Wedding Chapel**, for the privilege of driving through their "Tunnel of Love" in your own vehicle – plus at least $50 for the minister, and more for any flowers and music.

Beyond the bare essentials, the possibilities are infinite. Obvious extras include limousine service, formal wedding gowns and tuxedos, and accessories such as garters and boutonniers. Then there are the only-in-Vegas entertainment options, such as hiring an Elvis impersonator – most chapels have one or more on tap, typically costing upwards of $200 – to walk the bride down the aisle, serenade the happy couple, or even perform the ceremony. Other chapels in Vegas include **Chapel of the Flowers**, **Graceland Wedding Chapel**, **Little Church of the West**, **Mon Bel Ami Wedding Chapel**, **Viva Las Vegas Wedding Chapels**, and **A Special Memory**.

Anything that you can dream up for your wedding, Las Vegas will be happy to oblige. You can get married in the see-through underwater tunnel in Mandalay Bay's **Shark Reef Aquarium**; aboard a white wedding gondola on the Grand Canal in The Venetian (see pp16–17); or even beside the Colorado River at the bottom of the Grand Canyon, having flown there with **Sundance Helicopters** (see p129).

LGBTQ+ Weddings

When same-sex marriage was declared legal in Nevada in 2014, obliging the Marriage License Bureau to start issuing licenses to same-sex couples, it triggered something of a gold rush for the city's in-casino and stand-alone wedding chapels. The wedding options for same-sex couples are limitless, and include some chapels dedicated specifically to LGBTQ+ clients, including the **Gay Chapel of Las Vegas**.

Photography

The price of your wedding photos or video can form a major component of the overall cost of the ceremony. It is not unusual for a wedding chapel to forbid guests and participants from bringing their own cameras. Instead, you will have to use the chapel's own photographers, and pay for each individual print or copy.

DIRECTORY

LAS VEGAS WEDDINGS

Clark County Marriage License Bureau
MAP K4 ■ 201 E. Clark Ave
℡ 702 671 0600
w clarkcountynv.gov

WEDDING CEREMONIES

Office of Civil Marriages
MAP K4 ■ 330 S. 3rd St
℡ 702 671 0577
w clarkcountynv.gov

COSTS AND OPTIONS

A Little White Wedding Chapel
MAP L4 ■ 1301 Las Vegas Blvd S.
℡ 702 382 5943
w alittlewhitechapel.com

A Special Memory
MAP K4 ■ 800 South 4th St
℡ 702 637 4531
w aspecialmemory.com

Chapel of the Flowers
MAP L3 ■ 1717 Las Vegas Blvd S.
℡ 702 735 4331
w littlechapel.com

Graceland Wedding Chapel
MAP K4 ■ 619 Las Vegas Blvd S.
℡ 702 382 0091
w gracelandchapel.com

Little Church of the West
MAP C5 ■ 4617 Las Vegas Blvd S.
℡ 702 739 7971
w littlechurchlv.com

Mon Bel Ami Wedding Chapel
MAP K4 ■ 607 Las Vegas Blvd S.
w monbelami.com

Shark Reef Aquarium
MAP R1 ■ Mandalay Bay, 3950 Las Vegas Blvd S.
℡ 702 632 4555
w sharkreef.com

Viva Las Vegas Wedding Chapels
MAP L4 ■ 1205 Las Vegas Blvd S.
w vivalasvegas weddings.com

LGBTQ+ WEDDINGS

Gay Chapel of Las Vegas
MAP L4 ■ 1205 Las Vegas Blvd S.
w gaychapeloflas vegas.com

Gambling in Las Vegas

The Basics

Do not come expecting to make a fortune. With a combined annual income of more than $10 billion from gaming, the casinos have the advantage; they know this and aim to keep you playing for as long as possible. Before you start, decide on an amount that you can afford to lose and stick to it. In almost every instance, no matter what the game, the casino has a built-in "edge" – the longer you play, the more likely the casino will end up with your money. That, after all, is the whole principle on which this preposterous (but endlessly exciting) city came to be built.

There are several very simple ways in which casinos make money from gamblers. First comes the intrinsic edge in the games themselves. This is at its most obvious in roulette, the game in which a successful bet on a number from 1 to 36 is paid off with 36 times your original stake, although in fact there are either 37 (on a single-zero table) or 38 (on the much more common double-zero table) possible outcomes.

On top of that, the rules of play are esentially rigged; because, for example, the dealer always has the last turn in black-jack, the casino can win without the dealer's hand ever having to be played.

Apart from those two points, the frenzied atmosphere of the casino floor is hardly a place to make financial decisions, particularly with alcohol flowing freely. Gamblers are always liable to play poorly and make mistakes. Thus several casinos are happy to provide gamblers with the so-called "basic strategy" in blackjack – a computer-generated system that sets out exactly what a player should do in any specific circumstance – because they know that almost no player has the will-power to stick to a boring, rigid system instead of following sudden "hunches."

To improve your chances of success, take regular breaks rather than gambling nonstop. Gambling can be a mentally and physically exhausting activity. If you spend more than an hour deciding whether to "hold 'em" or "fold 'em," or 2 hours hunched over a slot machine, fatigue could well set in. Beware too, of the free alcoholic drinks offered by some casinos after you've placed a minimum bet, which may lead to poor gambling choices.

And finally, just supposing you do get lucky, be sensible about how you react. Be careful not to boast about your winnings in any place where there is a chance strangers might hear you.

Rules and Etiquette

Gamblers at all table games use plastic chips as opposed to cash. You join a game by taking up a vacant seat and "buying in" – exchanging your cash with the dealer for the equivalent quantity of plastic chips.

There is a sign at every table announcing the "minimum bet" allowed for the current game. These minimum amounts vary from table to table, from casino to casino, and from neighborhood to neighborhood – so, mini-mum bets are typically lower in Downtown Las Vegas than they are on the Strip, lower at casinos like Circus Circus (see p81) than at Bellagio (see pp14–15), and lower in the public areas of Bellagio than in its roped-off high-rollers' rooms. The minimum bets also vary according to the time of day; you will find they are much lower at 11am on a Monday morning than they are at midnight on a Saturday. Always ensure you know the current min-imum bet, and under-stand how it works for the game. For example, if there is a $10 minimum bet at roulette, you can make ten separate bets of $1 per spin, while a $10 minimum on blackjack obliges you to stake at least $10 per hand, no matter how many hands you are playing.

While the casinos of Las Vegas are relaxed in terms of how gamblers are dressed, and they are more than happy to ply them with drinks, visitors are nonetheless expected to behave appropriately. Try to touch your cards as little as possible when playing blackjack, for example, and in all games you should not attempt to touch or move your stake once play is underway. Note that on table games, it is customary to tip the dealer following a sizable win.

Underage Gambling

It is illegal in the state of Nevada for anyone under the age of 21 to gamble. Minors who are caught gambling are either arrested or given a citation, and could potentially face six months in jail. What is more, if you win a jackpot and you are not carrying the ID to prove that you are over 21, you will not even be allowed to keep your winnings.

Slot Clubs and Players Clubs

Anyone who comes to Las Vegas intending to spend any significant length of time gambling should sign up for the "slot club" or "players club." These clubs exists in each and every casino. Membership of these clubs is free, and it enables you to accumulate points by using a plastic card every time you bet on the slots or on the table games. Ultimately, these points can be exchanged for meals at restaurants and discounts on hotel rooms (or even, in some instances, free hotel rooms), as well as for more mundane items such as mugs, T-shirts, and baseball caps. Couples who are visiting Las Vegas on a joint trip should sign up for the clubs together, in order to receive two cards that earn points credited to the same shared account.

Aiming for the Jackpot

Slot machines in the major casinos are coinless; generally you feed notes in, and will be credited with the appropriate number of plays accordingly.

When playing at the slot machines, try to look for those that offer the best payback ratios (average percentage that the machine pays back to the player). Casinos like to be able to advertise themselves as having the "loosest" (highest-paying) slots, and so tend to have at least a few better-paying slots – often with signs stating "95 Per cent Slots" or some such slogan – scattered amid lower-paying machines. A slot machine in a higher denomination, such as $5, will usually offer a higher return than, say, a 25-cent machine, because the casino makes a higher rate of profit from a $5 spin than it does from one of 25 cents.

In addition, choose slot machines that offer the best payout schedules – displays on the front of each machine show the payout for each winning combination, and these can vary considerably. Bear in mind that the highest jackpots tend only to be available to those who play the maximum number of "lines" that each slot machine allows.

Never fall for the "It's due to hit" myth. Some gamblers imagine that a slot machine that has not paid any jackpots for a long time is due for a win. This is not necessarily true. Each spin of the reels is an independent event and has nothing to do with what has gone before or will come after.

Gaming Tournaments

Keen players choose to arrange their visits to coincide with the gaming tournaments that take place year-round in Las Vegas. These tournaments are devoted to poker, video poker, slots, and blackjack. Full schedules are available on the casino websites.

The most popular are the poker tournaments. These range from the contests hosted in nearly every casino each day (almost all casinos play "No-limit Hold 'Em," with an initial buy-in for each player of between $35 and $75) via assorted three- or four-day tournaments, up to the annual World Series of Poker, which takes over the Rio Casino for seven weeks between the months of May and July. The champion of the World Series of Poker wins around $10 million.

Blackjack tournaments are also common. They generally consist of three rounds, with the winners advancing to semifinals and finals. The entry fee usually covers a certain number of tournament chips, which are issued at the start and again before the semifinal and final rounds begin.

Participants in multi-day tournaments can expect to have a good deal of free time in between rounds; actual play takes up only 2 or 3 hours per day.

General Index

Acknowledgments

Author

Connie Emerson has lived in Nevada for more than 30 years, and writes travel articles for national and international publications.

Additional contributor
Greg Ward

Publishing Director Georgina Dee

Publisher Vivien Antwi

Design Director Phil Ormerod

Editorial Michelle Crane, Rebecca Flynn, Rachel Fox, Freddie Marriage, Fíodhna Ní Ghríofa, Scarlett O'Hara, Sally Schafer, Sophie Wright

Cover Design Maxine Pedliham, Vinita Venugopal

Design Tessa Bindloss, Richard Czapnik

Picture Research Phoebe Lowndes, Susie Peachey, Ellen Root, Lucy Sienkowska, Oran Tarjan

Cartography Suresh Kumar, Casper Morris, Reetu Pandey, John Plumer

Senior Production Editor Jason Little

Production Linda Dare

Factchecker Bob Barnes

Proofreader Alyse Dar

Indexer Kathryn O'Donoghue

Illustrator Chris Orr & Associates

First edition created by Blue Island Publishing, London

Revisions team Parnika Bagla, Christopher P Baker, Marta Bescos, Subhashree Bharati, Bharti Karakoti, Shikha Kulkarni, Suresh Kumar, Meghna, Chhavi Nagpal, George Nimmo, Garima Pandey, Bandana Paul, Rada Radojicic, Akshay Rana, Lucy Richards, Ankita Sharma, Rituraj Singh, Beverly Smart, Mark Silas, Manjari Thakur, Priyanka Thakur, Rachel Thompson, Stuti Tiwari, Vinita Venugopal, Åsa Westerlund, Tanveer Zaidi

Commissioned Photography Demetrio Carrasco, Dave King, Alan Keohane, Russell MacMasters, Oliver Perez, Rough Guides/ Greg Ward

Picture Credits

Freemont Street Experience: 23tl.

Getty Images: David Becker 60tl, 62t; Corbis Entertainment / Evan Hurd Photography 85tl; Eugene Robert Richee 37br; Icon Sportswire 44b.

Golden Nugget: 95br.

Grand Canyon National Park Lodges: 120tl.

Grand Canyon Railway: 31tl.

iStockphoto.com: somchaij 1; tobiasjo 88-89

Kemo Sabe: 21bc.

MGM Resorts International: 50cl, 65cl, 71crb, 14br, 41cr, 42clb, 58tl, 69tl; ARIA 57t, Cirque du Soleil Inc., Costumes by Dominique Lemieux 13tl.

Original Pancake House: 103br.

Palms Las Vegas: 64b.

Robert Harding Picture Library: Kord 77cl; Michael Weber 16br, 22bc.

Shutterstock.com: Kit Leong 39t

Station Casinos: 100t.

SuperStock: age fotostock 32-3; F1 Online 48-9.

Voodoo Zipline: 99cl.

Paul Wilkinson Collection: 30clb.

Wynn Las Vegas: Barbara Kraft 18br, 43tl, 47t, 64tl, 71tl; Tomasz Rossa 47crb.

Cover

Front and spine: **iStockphoto.com:** somchaij.
Back: **Alamy Stock Photo:** Cavan Images tl, lucky-photographer tr, SV cla; **AWL Images:** LEMAIRE Stephane crb; **iStockphto.com:** somchaij b.

Pull Out Map Cover

iStockphoto.com: somchaij.

All other images © Dorling Kindersley
For further information see:
www.dkimages.com

Penguin
Random
House

First Edition 2002

First published in Great Britain
by Dorling Kindersley Limited
DK, One Embassy Gardens, 8 Viaduct
Gardens, London, SW11 7BW, UK

The authorised representative in the EEA
is Dorling Kindersley Verlag GmbH.
Arnulfstr. 124, 80636 Munich, Germany

Published in the United States by
DK Publishing, 1745 Broadway, 20th Floor,
New York, NY 10019, USA

Copyright © 2002, 2022
Dorling Kindersley Limited

A Penguin Random House Company

23 24 25 10 9 8 7 6 5 4 3

**Reprinted with revisions 2003, 2005,
2007, 2009, 2011, 2013, 2015, 2016,
2018, 2020, 2022**

A CIP catalog record is available
from the British Library.

A catalog record for this book is available
from the Library of Congress.

ISSN 1479-344X
ISBN 978 0 2415 6609 1

Printed and bound in Malaysia

www.dk.com

*As a guide to abbreviations in visitor information blocks: **Adm** = admission charge; **L** = lunch.*

MIX
Paper | Supporting
responsible forestry
FSC www.fsc.org **FSC™ C018179**

This book was made with Forest
Stewardship Council™ certified
paper – one small step in DK's
commitment to a sustainable future.
**For more information go to
www.dk.com/our-green-pledge**